TERMS

in Their

Propositional Contexts

in Wittgenstein's

TRACTATUS

AN INDEX

TERMS
in Their
Propositional Contexts
in Wittgenstein's
TRACTATUS

AN INDEX

by

George Kimball Plochmann

and

Jack B. Lawson

Southern Illinois University Press

The profound difficulties in the interpretation of most philosophic texts make the use of indexes, concordances, glossaries, not
to mention commentaries, introductions, and notes all but essential
for student and scholar. When kings build, says Schiller, there is
plenty of work for carters. In particular, the fine-cut distinctions,
strange vocabulary, and subtle variations of terminology in Ludwig
Wittgenstein's Tractatus Logico-Philosophicus are of a sort that bring
not only the occasional but also the determined and well-prepared
reader to desperation. In this Index we do not propose to give the
solution to a single one of the difficulties in the Tractatus; but if
some means of finding the materials for solving those difficulties
are not at hand in the present little work, we shall be keenly dis-
appointed.

The Index is in English, if for no other reason than that we believe that there will be more readers of the text in that language
than in Wittgenstein's native tongue. Despite his long sojourn in
England, he evidently continued to think mainly in German--certainly
most of his texts are written out in German. But it has been no more
than a question of time before all these texts are Englished when
they are put into book form.

Wittgenstein used many words in a Germanic form virtually the
same as in English, words having Greek or Latin roots and remaining
unchanged, or nearly so, in both modern languages: das Mystische,
die Relation, die Grammatik. Finding a translation for these is, of
course, no great matter. Nor is there much trouble with such common
words as die Erfahrung, which almost without question goes into experience. But many of his important terms, those most characteristic-
ally his, are extremely difficult to put into English, either because
the German seems not to possess any precise equivalent in the latter
language (as with Gegenstand, ordinarily translated as object, but
which has a special twist, as being something standing over against),
or because Wittgenstein himself placed these terms in rather unusual
contexts, altering what they ordinarily mean, even making them appear
ambiguous. We have in mind such words as Sachlage, commonly rendered
state of affairs by C. K. Ogden, the first translator of the Tractatus, though this disconnects the word from Sache, entity, another
word used for object or thing. Wittgenstein had obviously intended
his two words to belong together; though they are not synonymous,
their common root must somehow be brought out. Then again there is
Sachverhalt, usually translated atomic fact, though a Sachverhalt is
not really always existent as a fact would have to be: there can be
a negative Sachverhalt. Moreover, -verhalt in this word has a meaning
of relationship completely neglected in atomic fact. Lastly, atomic
fact and state of affairs and object seem much farther apart in English than Sachverhalt, Sachlage, and Sache. Had Wittgenstein himself
wished to separate these three notions, he could have found plenty
of German words to hand.

There is one trick of style which makes the reader think that the
author of the Tractatus was not being careful about his terminology
after all: in many instances we find two words, one with a classical
root, such as Relation, the other of Teutonic origin, Beziehung, which
are almost impossible to render by more than one English word. At the

vi   risk of slight confusion, we have sometimes put such pairs into the
same words in English. It is quite true that the old translation
sometimes fails to separate unsinnig, nonsensical, and sinnlos,
senseless, where Wittgenstein intended anything but the same by these;
but the principle of using a separate word in our language for each
word in his can also be carried too far.

This Index follows a pattern differing slightly from the usual
ones, and does not attempt to group Wittgenstein's ideas under head-
ings other than those he himself supplies, as would, for example, the
elaborate Syntopicon printed in the Great Books of the Western World,
in which the writings of many types of philosophers are all indexed
together under common, and frequently distorting, rubrics. In our
work, all main entries are alphabetized, using no new language, and
the individual phrases stick, with few exceptions, as closely as possible to the original text, rewording only for the sake of clearer
emphasis or shortening. There is a peculiar kind of dialectical pro-
gression in the development of the chief terms in the Tractatus,
hence it is advisable to break up Wittgenstein's own order in using
them as little as possible; from that order one should be able to
learn much of how he employed his words in narrow and then again in
broad senses, in his own tightly, oddly restricted ways, and then in
loose, current ones. In reading the complete Tractatus, the variety
of detail militates against discerning the order of development in
the propositions. One has only to turn to the literature on the book
to see how seldom the careful recovery of the succession of meanings
has been tried. Some of the most recent studies are happy exceptions
to this generalization.

The length of this book has been considerably increased by our
having given nearly all citations fully enough so that a further
reference to the English text is not immediately needed in order to
make sense of Wittgenstein's usages. This is intended, then, as an
index to the problems and propositions rather than to the words and
names. Yet--and this is our strongest insistence--the present Index
will do an ill service if it encourages anyone to turn away from
rather than toward the text of the Tractatus itself. Several years
ago, one Paris designer who had got up a collection of dresses con-
sisting of a few straps and little more, said that he conceived of
clothing as but an indication of the health and beauty of the body.
Well, even a full translation--which in a way implies and is implied
by our Index--would have no more than referential value to the original German, and could never be an equivalent. Moreover, the order of
the propositions themselves in the text is of surpassing importance,
and our Index inevitably alters this beyond recognition. And there
is the editorial point that unfortunately, and despite long efforts,
errors were bound to creep into a list of references as lengthy as
this one, and we must do penance even ahead of time for the fact that
corrections no doubt remain to be made.

It is ironical to think that in future the number of books like
this one will quite probably increase greatly, and at the same time
the number of persons engaged in producing them will markedly di-
minish. A decade or two hence, it is more than likely that machines
will be scanning the pages of the classics (of which the Tractatus
is, we believe, one) and draw up by prearrangement a full index,
without errors, then translate it. It would have been reassuring to
have had a machine of this sort to check our mistakes. But the very
perfection of this new method, when it is at last developed, will
leave the problem of thinking untouched, just as--so says Wittgen-
stein--all the statements of fact skirt round the problem of life.
What Professor Entwhistle so unblinkingly said, that the answer to
a pitching machine is a batting machine, is scarcely bearable. What
we gained in the devising of this Index, in the working out of certain types of philosophical and philological problems raised in or
by it, is much more than we could have got by being handed the per-
fected, well-licked offspring of a computer. And so we come almost

full circle back to our first point: the ancillary books that hang
on a difficult text are valuable and even quite necessary; but one
of the greatest values of the original text is that it was so
elliptical to begin with, so seemingly ambiguous, so outright tough,
that it made its dependent commentaries necessary. The day when all
the apparent gaps in Plato or in Aristotle get plugged up and the
disagreements are settled will be the day when the canals of Venice
too are filled in, and the scurry of Paris and New York is quieted;
and then the challenge and fascination of philosophy will have taken
leave of us for good.

ACKNOWLEDGMENTS

Funds and free time for carrying out this project have been made available by Southern Illinois University, and for this we should like to thank Willis Moore, Chairman of the Department of Philosophy, Raymond H. Dey, Dean of the Division of Extension, John O. Anderson and David T. Kenney of the Graduate Office, and finally, and as always, Charles D. Tenney, Vice President for Instruction.

Valuable aid in preparing the Bibliography has been furnished by Beatrice Ann Stegeman, who checked through hundreds of journal issues; and by Geraldine Pittman. We cannot forget the innumerable occasions upon which help has been proffered by Alan M. Cohn and Earl Tannenbaum, Humanities Division, the University Libraries, in tracking down references and securing journals and books.

Annaliese Solderer Hanebrink has checked the German forms throughout.

To Vernon A. Sternberg, Director, the University Press, we owe much for his severe advice - and hearty encouragement.

Jo Ann D. Lawson has given much help in checking entries on the Index, and Carolyn Gassan Plochmann has read several versions of the introductory statements and made many suggestions.

The senior author has had freedom for normal - using this word in a broad sense, to be sure - teaching duties to work on this project and others connected with Wittgenstein by reason of a fellowship granted for 1960 by the John Simon Guggenheim Memorial Foundation, and to this organization thanks are cheerfully given.

We wish also to thank Messrs. Routledge and Company, Ltd., present holders of the copyright of the Tractatus Logico-Philosophicus, for answering the question, whether they had any objection to our proceeding with this Index, in the negative.

The principal typing of various drafts of this material was done by Kenneth E. Odum, seconded by Patricia A. Feeley, Charlotte Baczewski, Carolyn J. Sutton, Marcella Schaefer, and Phyllis McAfoos. Final preparation of the typescript was by Gloria Stokes and Patricia Ann Mason.

G.K.P.
J.B.L.

CONTENTS

NOTE ON THE INDEX

The entries follow an alphabetical order in the English words which we have (sometimes rather arbitrarily) selected as translations of the originals. The reader is invited to consult the German Word-list, if he is familiar with the original, to be sure where to look for our English equivalents. For certain of the principal entries we have written brief introductory paragraphs, chiefly to explain points of translation. Although we have exercised some independence in rendering words already rather standardized, still a book of the present sort is scarcely one where we wish to start fights, so we simply list here the words for which our renderings are most likely to seem controversial, and hope that the reader will note our explanations as they appear along the way in the Index:

Wirklichkeit - actuality; Fall - case; Erklärung - clarification; Zusammenhang - coherence; Tatsache - derivative fact; bezeichnet - designated; Bild - image; Sachverhalt - prime fact; eigentlich - proper; Urbild - proto-image; sinnvoll - sense-bearing; Bestehen - subsistence; Verbindung - union

In general, words have been included only when they seem to us to serve a definite philosophical purpose in Wittgenstein's text. Some words, such as appearance, cause, create, and the like, are given almost no philosophical weight to bear, however often they may have been made crucial terms in other writers. Some of these words have been included to remind our readers that among the most important clues to understanding the Tractatus is the list of what is played down, or even omitted. On the other hand, there is no obvious limit to this, and overzealousness could only clutter up the Index. And there is a story to which Wittgenstein refers (in 4.014) about the two youths, the lilies, and the horses which are in a certain respect one. We have sent these packing. So with a number of similar items.

We have, in the interests of dialectic, kept together in single entries the singular and plural nouns, for between the use of these there is rarely an important philosophical distinction in the Tractatus (as there would be between mind and minds, god and gods in some of the Greek writers); adjectival and adverbial forms, on the other hand, and tenses of verbs, their participles and voices, are in general separated.

In (parentheses) one will find alternative translations of the chief terms, at any rate translations which have had some currency in the C. K. Ogden edition, less often, and considering the date of its publication and our writing, by coincidence, in that of Peers and McGuinness, or in commentators. We place in [brackets] the German equivalents as they appear in the original text. Cross-references are scattered pretty liberally throughout the Index. Titles of books, the dedication, motto, and footnote have not been indexed.

We have included a few symbols, like aRb and "A says p," in the English list, simply because recent literature has had quite a bit to say about them. Nearly all the formulas and other notational expressions, with some trivial exceptions, appear in the List of Symbols.

xiv   A word about the phrasing of the statements. We have in many, many cases translated as exactly as we could the words of the original, and after that rearranged them in some way so as better to bring out the meaning of the term being indexed. Occasionally a device so slender as an inverted word order will throw a little more light on a term, even though Wittgenstein himself rarely paused to employ this in the original. At any rate, it would be risky, indeed most risky, to quote any lines in our Index without first verifying that they appear <u>as we have them</u>, in the original. A number of propositions marked with * have been stated here in such a way that the reader will definitely need to consult the text. In most of these Wittgenstein has given technical formulations which cannot well be condensed and which make use of symbols.

TERMS
in Their
Propositional Contexts
in Wittgenstein's
TRACTATUS

AN INDEX

"A"

    3.203   "A" is the same sign as "A"

A priori

    2.225   no image true a priori

    3.04   an a priori true thought is one whose possibility conditions its truth

    3.05   an a priori true thought could be recognized only through the thought itself

    5.133   all deduction takes place a priori

    5.4731   that logic is a priori consists in this, that we cannot think unlogically

    5.55   a priori answer regarding all possible elementary propositions must be given

    5.5541   a priori decision possible whether a 27-member relation is needed

    5.5571   nonsense to try to give elementary propositions a priori

    5.634   no part of our experience is a priori; no order of things a priori either

    6.31   so-called law of induction not a priori

    6.3211   a priori certainty is purely logical

    6.33   possibility of a logical form known a priori

    6.34   propositions such as law of causality are a priori insights into possible forms of scientific propositions

    6.35   properties of network describing world are given a priori

aRb

    3.1432   we must say "That 'a' stands in a certain relation to 'b' says that aRb" rather than "The complex sign 'aRb' says 'a stands in relation R to b'"

    4.012   proposition of form aRb perceived as image

*   4.1252   aRb as member of series of propositions ordered by an internal relation

4   A says p [A sagt p]. See also Judge

       5.542   "A says p" is of form "'p' says p," and gives a
               co-ordination of derivative facts through a co-
               ordination of their objects

      A thinks p [A denkt p]

       5.541   "A thinks p" and similar expressions superficially
               appear to contain one proposition in another

       5.542   "A thinks p" is clearly of form "'p' thinks p"

      Abstract [abstrakt]

       5.5563 Wittgenstein's problems are not abstract

      Accident [Zufall]

       2.0121 if a state of affairs were fitted to an independent
               thing, this would be an accident

       6.1232 propositions like Axiom of Reducibility could be true
               only by accident

       6.3   outside logic all is accident

      Accidental [zufallig]

       2.012   in logic nothing is accidental

       3.34   proposition has essential and accidental features;
               latter are connected with propositional sign

       5.4733 common sign for different symbols is accidental

       6.031   generality in mathematics not accidental

       6.1232 logical general validity contrasted with accidental
               general validity

       6.41   all happening and being-so is accidental; what makes
               world not accidental must lie outside world

      Accidentally [zufalligerweise]

       6.1231 generality means to be valid accidentally for all
               things

      Accord (harmony) [Einklang]

       6.363   induction is process of assuming simplest law we can
               bring into accord with experience

      Action [Handlung]

       6.422   consequence of actions irrelevant to ethics; ethical
               reward and punishment for an action must lie within
               action itself

      Action (effect) [Wirkung]

       6.321   in mechanics, law of least action is a minimum-law

Action (effect) [Wirkung] continued

    6.3211   men believed that there must be a law of least action
            before knowing how it went

Activity [Tätigkeit]

    4.112   philosophy not a doctrine but an activity

Actual (real) [wirklich]
    ("Actual" improves on "real" because the latter implies some
    kind of ontological subsistence, some ultimacy of existence,
    while the former connotes better the temporary springing into
    being of patterns of connectivity which Wittgenstein calls
    facts - of various kinds - and states of affairs.)

    2.022   actual world and imaginary world have form in common

    4.0031   apparent logical form of proposition need not be
            actual one

    4.431   difficulties in Frege's view that true and false are
            actual objects

    5.461   use of brackets with apparent proto-signs shows that
            these are not actual proto-signs

Actuality (reality) [Wirklichkeit]. See also Reality; State of
    Affairs
    ("Reality" conveys a sense of wholeness foreign to Wittgen-
    stein's insistence upon the this, the individual, as the
    subject of the proposition; "actuality" is the better trans-
    lation. We save "reality" to translate Realität.)

    2.06   actuality is existence and non-existence of prime
           facts

    2.063   total actuality is the world

    2.12   image a model of actuality

    2.1511   image is tied to actuality

    2.1512   image is like a measuring stick laid against actuality

    2.1515   co-ordinations are feelers of image touching actuality

    2.17   image has form of representation in common with
           actuality

    2.171   image can image every actuality whose form it has

    2.18   image has logical form in common with actuality;
           logical form is form of actuality

    2.201   image images actuality by representing a possibility
           of the subsistence and non-subsistence of prime facts

    2.21   image agrees with actuality or not; is true or false

    2.222   agreement of sense of image with actuality constitutes
           truth or falsehood

6   Actuality (reality) [Wirklichkeit] continued

Actually [wirklich]

Addition [Addition]

    5.2341   logical addition is an operation

Addition Sign [Additionszeichen]

    5.02   addition sign for cardinal numbers in Russell's nota-
             tion a matter of arbitrary agreement

Adjective [Eigenschaftswort]

    3.323   in colloquial language same word can be both proper
             name and adjective

Adjustments. See Stipulations

Aesthetics [Aesthetik]

    6.421   ethics and aesthetics are one

Affirm [bejahen]

    5.124   a proposition affirms every proposition following
             from it

  * 5.513   what is common to all symbols which affirm both p
             and q is "p . q" etc.

    5.514   in firmly established notation is rule for construct-
             ing all propositions which affirm p or q

Affirmation [Bejahung]

    4.064   affirmation cannot give a proposition sense, as sense
             is what the proposition affirms

    5.44   the possibility of denial is prejudged in affirmation

    6.231   affirmation can be conceived as double denial

Agree [stimmen]

    2.21   image agrees with actuality or not

    3.24   complex can only be given by description, and this
             will agree or not agree

    3.411   geometrical and logical locus are both possibilities
             of an existence

Agree [zusammenfallen]. See Coincide

Agreement [Stimmen]

  * 5.512   how negation can bring proposition into agreement with
             actuality explained

Agreement [Übereinkunft]

    3.315   class of values for variable proposition depends on

8   Agreement [Übereinkunft] continued

        arbitrary agreement about parts of proposition which is made variable, but existence of such class depends on no agreement

    5.02   where way of symbolizing depends on arbitrary agreement, simple sign could be used as well as complex

Agreement [Übereinstimmung]

    2.222   truth of proposition is its agreement with actuality

    4.2   agreement or disagreement with possibilities of subsistence or non-subsistence of a prime fact is sense of a proposition

    4.4   proposition an expression of agreement with truth-possibilities of elementary propositions

  * 4.42   number of possibilities of agreement of a proposition with truth-possibilities of elementary propositions given

  * 4.43   means of expressing agreement with truth-possibilities of schema

    4.431   agreement with truth-possibilities of elementary propositions expresses truth-conditions of the proposition

    4.462   conditions of agreement with world--the representing relations--cancel in tautology

All (everything) [alle]. See also Totality

    1.   world is all that is the case

    1.11   world is determined by derivative facts and by their being all

    1.12   totality of derivative facts determines what is the case and all that is not the case

    1.21   any derivative fact can be the case independently of all others

    2.0121   all possibilities are the derivative facts of logic

    5.521   concept "all" separate from truth-function

    5.634   all that we see could be otherwise; all that we can describe could be otherwise

All-embracing [allumfassend]

    5.511   the all-embracing, world-mirroring logic uses special snags and manipulations

Alphabetic Writing [Buchstabenschrift]

    4.016   alphabetic writing came from hieroglyphic writing

Alphabetic Writing [Buchstabenschrift] continued

      without loss of essence of imaging

Altering [wechselnd]

    2.0271   the configuration is altering, not the object

Analogous [analog]

    4.1121   danger for Wittgenstein's method analogous to un-
            essential psychological investigations in studies of
            thought-processes

Analogue [Analoge]

    4.441   an analogue to the lack of corresponding objects
           for T and F holds for all signs which express same
           as schemata of T and F

    6.3611   description of spatial sequence of events is an
            analogue to description of temporal sequence

Analysis [Analyse]

    3.25   only one complete analysis of the proposition

    3.442   sign of complex not arbitrarily resolved in analysis

    4.221   analysis of propositions must ultimately come to
           elementary propositions

Analyzed [analysiert]. See also Dismembered; Divided; Taken to
            Pieces

    3.201   a proposition is fully analyzed when elements of
           propositional sign correspond to objects of our
           thoughts

Analytic [analytisch]

    6.11   propositions of logic are analytic

Ancients [Alten]

    6.372   ancients stopped short at God and Fate; were clearer
           than moderns

Answer [Antwort]

    6.5   for an answer which cannot be expressed, the question
           cannot be either

    6.51   a question exists only where there is an answer

    6.52   no scientific answers touch problem of life; the
           answer is that no question is left

Anumerical [zahllos]

    4.128   logical forms are anumerical

Applied [angewandt]

    3.5   the applied, thought-of propositional sign is the
               thought

    6.123   one law of contradiction suffices for every "type"
               since it is not applied to itself

Arbitrarily [willkürlich]

    3.3442 sign of complex not resolved arbitrarily in analysis

Arbitrary [willkürlich]

    3.315   class of values for variable proposition depends on
               arbitrary agreement about parts of proposition which
               is made variable

    3.332   sign is arbitrary

    3.342   if something is arbitrary in notation, then something
               else is the case

    5.02   where way of symbolizing depends on arbitrary agree-
               ment, simple sign could be used as well as complex

    5.473   "Socrates is identical" is nonsensical because we
               have made no arbitrary determination of property
               "identical"

    5.47321 Occam's Razor is not an arbitrary rule

    5.554   statement of any special forms would be wholly arbi-
               trary

    6.124   in symbols there is much that is arbitrary, much that
               is not

Argument [Argument]

    3.333   function cannot be its own argument (Cf. 5.251)

    4.431   arguments not properly determined in Frege's explana-
               tion of the truth-concept

    5.02   easy to mistake arguments of functions for indices of
               names

    5.47   where there is composition, there is argument and
               function, and so all logical constants

    5.523   sign of generality occurs as an argument

    5.5351 nonsense for Russell to use p ⊃ p before propositions
               to show that arguments have correct form

    6.1203 truth of whole proposition co-ordinated with all truth-
               combinations of its argument

Arise [entstehen]

    3.324   fundamental confusions arise when same word designates

Assumption [Annahme] continued

    6.4312   assumption of temporal immortality inadequate

Assure [verbürgen]

    3.4   existence of logical locus assured by existence of
           constituents of proposition

Asymmetry [Asymmetrie]

* 6.3611   asymmetry and descriptions of causes which brings
           about one event rather than another

Atomic Fact. See Prime Fact

Attempt [Versuch]

    6.343   mechanics an attempt to construct all true proposi-
           tions needed for world description according to
           single plan

Axiom of Infinity (Eng.)

    5.535   Russell's Axiom of Infinity is meant to say that there
           are infinite names with different meanings; solution
           of problems arising from Axiom of Infinity

Axiom of Reducibility (Eng.)

    6.1232   Axiom of Reducibility not a logical proposition

    6.1233   world in which Axiom of Reducibility is not valid is
           imaginable

Axioms [Axiome]

    6.341   all propositions in world description must be obtained
           from mechanical axioms

-B-

Bases [Basen]

    5.21   internal relations of structures of propositions can
           be displayed by representing proposition as result of
           operation on other propositions (the bases of the
           operation)

    5.22   operation is expression of relation between structures
           of its result and its bases

    5.234   truth-functions of elementary propositions are results
           of operations having elementary propositions as bases

    5.24   what is common to bases and results of operation is
           bases themselves

14 Bases [Basen] continued

Bearer [Träger]

Beautiful [Schöne]

Being-so [So-Sein]

Believe [glauben]

Binding (connection) [Verband]. See also Combination; Union

Blue [blau]

Body [Körper]

Body [Leib]

Book [Buch]

Book [Buch] continued

    5.631   book on "world as I found it" would contain no mention of myself

Brackets [Klammern]

    4.441   no object corresponds to brackets in schemata

    4.442   in schemata of truth-conditions, number of places in left-hand bracket is determined by number of members in right-hand bracket

    5.2522   expression in brackets of general member of a formal series is a variable

    5.452   no new device can be introduced innocently in logic in brackets

    5.46   with introduction of action of all possible combinations of brackets the nature of proper general protosigns becomes clear

    5.461   that apparent relations like v and ⊃ need brackets is meaningful

*   5.501   sign given for expression in brackets whose members are propositions

    6.1203   brackets used to express truth-combinations

Break Up (divide) [zerfallen]

    1.2   the,world breaks up into derivative facts

Building [Gebäude]

    6.341   bricks must be given from which the building of science is made

-C-

Calculate [berechnen]

    6.126   whether proposition belongs to logic can be calculated from logical properties of symbol

Calculation [Rechnung]

    6.2331   process of calculation brings about necessary intuition for solution of mathematical problems; calculation is not an experiment

Capacity [Fähigkeit]

    4.002   man possesses capacity to construct languages which can express every sense

Case (what is the case, what turns out so, what is so, what happens   17
     to be) [Fall] continued

5.5542   what must be in order for anything to be the case--has
         this question sense?

5.61   that logic can exclude certain possibilities cannot be
         the case

6.1203   cases where no sign of generality occurs in tautology

6.23   whether it is the case that two expressions can be
         substituted one for another

6.342   as is the case, description of world by Newtonian
         mechanics says something about the world

6.3631   no grounds for believing that the simplest explanation
         will actually be the case

Causal Law [Kausalitätsgesetz]

6.32   causal law is no law, but the form of a law

6.321   causal law is a class name

6.36   if there were a causal law it might run: there are
         natural laws

6.362   what is excluded by causal law cannot be described

Causal Nexus [Kausalnexus]

5.136   no causal nexus to prove one state of affairs from
         another state of affairs

5.1361   belief in causal nexus is superstition

Causality [Kausalität]

5.1362   future actions could only be known if causality were
         an inner necessity, like logical proof

Cause [Ursache]

6.3611   of two events which mutually exclude each other, one
         can happen only if there is an asymmetry which itself
         is a cause

Cease [aufhören]

6.431   in death world does not change but ceases

Center [Mittelpunkt]

5.143   tautology is substanceless center of propositions

Certain [gewiss]

4.404   truth of tautology is certain

Circumstances [Umstände] continued

    5.154   all circumstances give equal probability to drawing of white or black ball from urn

    5.155   unit of probability proposition is: circumstances give to occurrence of a definite event such-and-such a degree of probability

Clarification (explanation) [Erklärung]
    (We adopt this translation to bring out one of Wittgenstein's fundamental notions, that of making clear. An explanation is an external description rather than an account of the internal properties and relations of a thing.)

    4.0412   idealist clarification inadequate for clarifying spatial relations

    4.063   black spot on white paper an image for clarification of concept of truth

  * 4.431   Frege's clarification of his ideography in terms of truth-conditions

    5.5422   correct clarification of form of proposition "A judges p"

    6.112   clarification of logical propositions must give them a unique place

    6.371   so-called natural laws as clarifications of phenomena an illusion

Clarification [Klärung]

    4.112   purpose of philosophy is the logical clarification of thoughts

Clarified (explained) [erklärt]

    3.263   meanings of proto-signs can be clarified through elucidations

    4.02   we understand sense of propositional sign without having it clarified (Cf. 4.021)

    4.026   meanings of simple signs must be clarified if we are to understand them

    5.5423   seeing cube in two ways clarified in that we see different derivative facts

Clarifying [Klarwerden]

    4.112   result of philosophy is the clarifying of propositions

Class [Klasse]

    3.142   a class of names cannot express a sense

20   Class [Klasse] continued

        3.311   an expression is a common characteristic mark of a
                 class of propositions

    *   3.315   how we form a class of propositions which are all
                 values of a variable proposition

        4.1272   formal concepts like "complex" represent variables,
                 not classes

        5.451   fundamental concepts must not be introduced first for
                 one class of cases, then for another

    Classes, Theory of. See Theory

    Classification [Klassifikation]

        5.454   no classification in logic

    Clear [klar]

        4.112   philosophy should make clear thoughts that are other-
                 wise turbid

        4.126   ground of confusion of formal concepts and proper con-
                 cepts is made clear

        5.45   construction of logic out of its proto-signs must be-
                 come clear

        5.46   with introduction of effect of all possible combina-
                 tions of brackets the nature of proper general proto-
                 signs becomes clear

        6.372   ancients were more clear than moderns insofar as they
                 recognized one clear conclusion

        6.521   after long doubt the sense of life, when finally clear,
                 cannot be expressed

    Clearly [klar]

        4.115   philosophy will mean the unsayable by clearly repre-
                 senting the sayable

        4.116   everything that can be thought can be clearly thought;
                 everything that can be said can be clearly said

    Clothe (disguise, costume) [verkleiden]

        4.002   language clothes the thought

    Clothed [bekleidet]

        4.002   from outer form of clothes one cannot infer form of
                 clothed thought

    Cognize (be acquainted with, know) [kennen]

        2.0123   to cognize an object means to cognize the collective
                 possibilities of its occurrence in prime facts

Cognize (be acquainted with, know) [kennen] continued

    2.01231 to cognize object means to cognize internal rather than external properties

Cohere (hang together) [zusammenhängen]

    2.032   way objects cohere in prime fact is its structure

    4.03   proposition essentially coheres with the state of affairs; the logical image is this coherence

Coherence (connection, combination, context) [Zusammenhang]
(We have used this word to imply a relation closer than any accidental "combination" or "connection".)

    2.0122   thing is independent, but this is its form of coherence, therefore dependence

    2.15   coherence of elements of picture is its structure

    3.3   name has meaning only in coherence of a proposition

    4.22   elementary proposition is a coherence of names

    4.23   name occurs in the proposition only in the coherence of elementary proposition

  * 5.1311 notation presented to make inner coherence of inferential sequence obvious

    5.1362 coherence of knowledge and known is logical necessity

    6.361   only coherences conforming to law are thinkable

    6.374   no logical coherence between world and will; no physical coherence either

Coincide (agree) [zusammenfallen]

    Foreword: How far Wittgenstein's efforts coincide with those of other philosophers a matter of indifference

    5.64   solipsism, strictly carried out, coincides with pure realism

Collective [sämtliche]

    2.0123   to cognize an object means to cognize the collective possibilities of its occurrence in prime facts

    2.02331 objects having their collective properties in common cannot be distinguished

Collide [kollidieren]

    5.557   logic may not collide with its application

Colloquial Language [Umgangsprache]

    3.323   in colloquial language same word can designate in different ways, etc.

22   Colloquial Language [Umgangsprache] continued

        4.002   colloquial language is part of human organism and not less complicated than it

        5.5563 propositions of colloquial language are in order, just as they are

Color [Farbe]

        2.0131 a speck in visual field must have color

        2.0251 color is a form of objects

        4.123   this color and that stand in internal relation to each other

        6.3751 two colors in one place logically impossible; logical structure of color excludes this possibility; that a point in visual field has two colors is a contradiction

Colored [färbig]

        2.171   image images everything that is colored

Coloredness [Färbigkeit]

        2.0251 coloredness is a form of objects

Colorless [farblos]

        2.0232 objects are colorless

Color-space [Farbenraum]

        2.0231 a speck in the visual field has the color-space around it

Combination [Kombination]

        4.27   all combinations of prime facts can exist

        4.28   to combinations of prime facts correspond same number of truth-possibilities of n elementary propositions

        4.442   rule of combination of truth-possibilities determines truth-conditions

        5.46   when right logical signs are introduced, the sense of all their combinations is introduced also

Combined [verhalten]. See Related

Common [gemein, gemeinsam]

        2.16   derivative fact, to be image, must have something in common with what is imaged

        2.18   image must have logical form in common with actuality to be able to image it

        2.2   image and imaged have logical form of imaging in common

Common [gemein, gemeinsam] continued   23

3.31   expressions are all essential for sense if propositions
            have them in common

3.311   expression is common characteristic mark of class of
            propositions

3.317   fixing of values of propositional variable is a de-
            claration of propositions whose common mark is the
            variable

3.321   two different symbols can have sign in common, but they
            designate in different ways

3.322   common mark of two objects cannot be a sign, which is
            arbitrary

3.333   common to arguments containing their own functions is
            a sign, which designates nothing

3.341   essential in proposition is what is common to all prop-
            ositions which can express the same sense

3.3411   if real name is what all symbols which designate ob-
            ject have in common, then no sort of composition is
            essential for a name

3.343   all correct symbolisms have in common that they are
            translatable one into another

3.344   expression of what is common to all notations for the
            truth-functions

3.3441   common to all notations that they can be replaced by
            ~p and p v q

4.014   logical structure is common to language and world

4.12   propositions cannot represent what they have in common
            with actuality - the logical form

5.143   contradiction is what is held in common in propositions
            which no proposition has in common with another; tauto-
            logy is what all propositions have in common which have
            nothing in common with one another

5.24   what is common to bases and results of operation is
            the bases themselves

5.47   the one logical constant is what all propositions
            have in common

5.4733   two symbols with different symbolizing relations
            have sign in common only by accident

5.512   what is common to all signs for denial of a proposi-
            tion; common rule for different signs of denial; what
            is common to denying proposition mirrors denial

5.513   what is common to all symbols affirming "and" or "or";

Complex [komplex] continued

    4.2211   even if world is infinitely complex, there are objects

    5.515   if p in p v q does not stand for complex sign, it
                cannot have a sense by itself

Complex [Komplex]

    2.0201   statements about complexes are analysable into state-
                ments about constituents

    3.24   proposition about a complex stands in internal rela-
                tions to proposition about its constituent; complex
                only given by description; proposition about non-
                existent complex is not nonsense, but false; we see
                that a propositional element designates a complex
                from an indeterminateness in propositions in which
                element occurs; combinations of symbols of complex
                into a simple sign can be expressed by a definition

    3.3442   sign of complex not arbitrarily resolved in analysis

    4.1272   word "complex" designates a formal concept and is
                represented by a variable

    4.441   complex of signs "T" and "F" corresponds to no ob-
                ject or complex of objects

    5.5423   perceiving a complex is perceiving such-and-such a
                relation of constituents

Complicated [kompliziert]

    4.002   colloquial speech not less complicated than human
                organism; silent stipulations to understand collo-
                quial language are complicated

    6.1262   proof in logic is only a mechanical device to faci-
                litate recognition of tautology where it is compli-
                cated

Composite (compound, composited) [zusammengesetzt]

    2.021   objects cannot be composite

    3.143   Frege would call proposition a composite name

    3.1431   conceiving the imaging proposition as a composite
                of spatial objects makes clear its essence

    4.032   proposition "ambulo" is composite of stem and ending

    5.5261   a fully generalized proposition is, like every other
                proposition, composite; composite symbol has some-
                thing in common with other symbols

    5.5421   composite soul not a soul

Concept (notion) [Begriff] continued

> 4.1273   concept "member of this formal series" is a formal concept
>
> 5.2523   concept of successive application of operation is equivalent to concept, "and so forth"
>
> 5.521   the concept "all" separate from truth-function
>
> 5.555   we have concept of elementary proposition apart from its special logical form
>
> 6.022   concept of number is what is common to all numbers; of equality what is common to special numerical equalities

Concept-Word [Begriffswort]

> 4.1272   "object" is incorrectly used as a proper concept-word; illusory propositions arise from its use

Concept-writing. See Ideography

Concept-number. See Number Concept

Conception (apprehension) [Auffassung]

> 4.062   conception of p as ~p in relation to true and false
>
> 4.1213   we feel we have correct logical conception if our sign-language is correct
>
> 6.25   even in old conception of logic we can give description of all "true" logical propositions at outset

Conclude. See Infer

Conclusion [Abschluss]

> 6.372   ancients clearer than moderns insofar as they recognized one clear conclusion

Conclusion [Schluss]

> 4.023   one can draw conclusions from a false proposition
>
> 5.152   certainty of logical conclusion is a limiting case of probability

Concrete [konkret]

> 5.5563   our problem not abstract but perhaps the most concrete there is

Condition [Bedingung]

> 4.41   truth-possibilities of elementary propositions are conditions of truth or falsehood of propositions
>
> 4.461   tautology true without truth-conditions; contradiction true on no condition

28   Condition [Bedingung] continued

      4.462   in tautology, conditions of agreement with world
             cancel one another

      4.463   truth-conditions determine elbowroom left to
             facts by proposition

      5.5422 Russell's theory (of A says "p") does not satisfy
             condition of showing impossibility of judging a
             nonsense

Configuration [Konfiguration]

      2.0231 configuration of objects first forms material
             properties of world

      2.0271 configuration is the alterable, unstable

      2.0272 configuration of objects is the prime fact

      3.21   configuration of simple signs corresponds to that
             of objects in state of affairs

Conforming to law [gesetzmässig]

      6.361   only connections conforming to law are thinkable

Conformity to Law (regularity) [Gesetzmässigkeit]

      6.3   investigation of logic means the investigation of
             all conformity to law

Confusion [Verwechslung]

      3.324   fundamental confusions arise from same signs
             which are really different symbols

      4.122   confusion between internal and external rela-
             tions widespread

      4.126   confusion of formal and proper concepts in old
             logic

Connection. See Binding

Conservation. See Law of Conservation

Consequent Propositions [Folgesätze]

      5.123   if God creates world in which certain proposi-
             tions are true, he thereby creates world in which all
             consequent propositions are true

Consequential [folgenschwer]

      5.452   introduction of new device in symbolism of logic
             must always be consequential

Consist [bestehen]

      3.14   propositional sign consists in definite relation
             of its elements

Consist [bestehen]   continued

4.112   philosophical work consists essentially of elucidations

4.22   elementary proposition consists of names

4.221   elementary propositions consist of names in immediate union

4.2211   even if every derivative fact consists of infinite number of prime facts, still there must be prime facts

5.1362   freedom of will consists in this, that future actions cannot be known now

5.4731   that logic is a priori consists in this, that nothing can be thought unlogically

5.55   elementary proposition consists of names

6.342   net of mechanics could consist of different sorts of figures

6.363   process of induction consists in assuming simplest law that can be made to harmonize with our experience

Constant [konstant]

3.312   expression is constant as it presupposes forms of all propositions in which it occurs

4.126   expression of formal concept is propositional variable in which only this characteristic feature is constant

4.1271   every variable represents a constant form

5.501   members of expression in brackets can be described by direct enumeration, setting constant values of expression

Constant [Konstante]

3.313   in limiting case, variables become constants

4.0312   logical constants do not stand as proxies for objects

5.4   there are no such things as "logical objects," "logical constants," in sense of Frege and Russell

5.441   instances cited of disappearance of apparent logical constants

5.47   the one logical constant is that which all propositions have in common with one another

5.522   sign of generality makes prominent the constants

Constituent (constituent part) [Bestandteil]

2.011   essential to thing that it can be a constituent of a prime fact

Construction [Konstruktion]

> 5.233   operation can first occur where logical construction of proposition begins

Contain [enthalten]

> 2.014   objects contain possibility of all states of affairs
>
> 2.203   image contains possibility of the state of affairs it represents
>
> 3.02   thought contains possibility of state of affairs which it thinks
>
> 3.24   notation for generality contains a proto-image
>
> 3.263   elucidations are propositions which contain proto-signs
>
> 3.333   functional sign contains proto-image of its argument and it cannot contain itself
>
> 4.063   that which "is true" must contain verb of proposition
>
> 4.1273   way Frege and Russell express some general propositions contains a vicious circle

Contained [enthalten]

> 3.13   in the proposition is contained possibility of expressing sense, not sense itself; form of sense is contained, not content of proposition
>
> 3.318   proposition is conceived as function of expressions contained in it
>
> 3.332   propositional sign cannot be contained in itself
>
> 5.121   when truth-grounds of one proposition are contained in truth-grounds of another, p follows from q

Containing [enthaltend]

> 5.02   we cognize meaning of containing sign from argument as much as from index

Content [Inhalt]

> 2.025   substance is form and content
>
> 3.13   "content of proposition" is the content of the sense-bearing proposition; content is not contained in proposition
>
> 3.31   expression marks a content

Continuity [Kontinuität]

> 6.34   law of continuity of nature and similar propositions are intuitions of possible forms of propositions of science

32   Contradict [widersprechen]

    4.1211   if two propositions contradict one another, this
              is shown from their structures; one elementary
              proposition cannot be contradicted by another

    5.1241   every proposition which contradicts another, denies
              it

    Contradiction [Kontradiktion]

    4.46   contradiction defined in terms of truth-possibili-
              ties

    4.461   contradiction shows that it says nothing; is under
              no conditions true; is senseless

    4.4611   contradiction not nonsensical, but part of symbo-
              lism

    4.462   contradiction not an image of actuality; allows
              no possible state of affairs

    4.463   contradiction fills whole logical space, and
              leaves no point to reality

    4.464   truth of contradiction impossible

    4.466   contradiction and tautology limiting cases of
              unities of signs

    4.4661   signs are combined in contradiction, but their
              relations are meaningless

    5.143   contradiction the external limit of propositions

    5.525   impossibility of a state of affairs expressed not
              by a proposition but by a contradiction

    6.1202   contradiction could be used to show structural
              properties of propositions, instead of tautolo-
              gies

    6.123   no special law of contradiction for every logical
              type

    6.3751   logical product of two elementary propositions
              cannot be a contradiction; assertion that point
              in visual field has two different colors is a
              contradiction

    Contradiction [Widerspruch]. See also Law of Contradiction

    4.211   sign of elementary proposition that no elemen-
              tary proposition can stand in contradiction to it

    6.123   contrary to what Russell supposed, no special law
              of contradiction for every "type"

    6.3751   principle of contradiction represented in physics
              so that particles in different places at same
              time cannot be identical

Contradictory [kontradiktorisch]

    4.46   when proposition is false for all truth-possibilities,
                 the truth-conditions are contradictory

Co-ordinate [zuordnen]

    4.43   agreement with truth-possibilities expressible by
                 co-ordinating T (true) with them

    5.526   one can completely describe world without co-ordina-
                 ting any name with a determined object

    6.1203   brackets used to co-ordinate truth of proposition
                 with all truth-combinations of its argument

Co-ordinated [koordiniert]

    5.64   I in solipsism shrinks to extensionless point and
                 there remains the reality co-ordinated with it

Co-ordinates [Koordinaten]

    3.032   figure contradicting space laws cannot be presented in
                 geometry by co-ordinates; nor a point which does not
                 exist

    3.41   logical locus is the propositional sign and the logi-
                 cal co-ordinates

Co-ordination [Koordination]

    3.42   denial, logical sum, etc., do not introduce new ele-
                 ments in co-ordination

Co-ordinations (orderings, attachments) [Zuordnungen]

    2.1514   imaging relation is the co-ordinations of elements of
                 image and things

    2.1515   co-ordinations of elements are their feelers touching
                 actuality

    4.44   sign arising from co-ordination of T (true) with
                 truth-possibilities is a propositional sign

    5.542   "A says p" a co-ordination of derivative facts through
                 co-ordinations of their objects

  * 6.1203   method of representing co-ordination of truth and
                 falsity with bracket-notation

Copula [Kopula]

    3.323   "is" appears as copula, sign of equality, and ex-
                 pression of existence

Correctness [Richtigkeit]

    6.2321   correctness of propositions of mathematics seen with-
                 out comparing what they express with derivative facts

34   Correspond [entsprechen]

2.13   objects correspond to elements in image

3.2   thoughts can be expressed in propositions so that objects of thoughts correspond to elements of propositional sign

3.21   configuration of objects in state of affairs corresponds to the configuration of simple signs in propositional signs

3.315   that class of values remains for variable proposition when all signs with arbitrarily determined meanings are made variable, corresponds to logical form

4.0621   that "p" and "~p" can say same thing shows that "~" corresponds to nothing in actuality, though these propositions have opposite senses

* 4.063   image to explain concept of truth developed by pointing out what corresponds to what in white paper with black spot and concept of truth; to proposition without sense corresponds nothing

4.1121   Wittgenstein's study of sign-language corresponds to study of thought processes

4.123   to shifting use, in example, of "property" and "relation" corresponds shifting use of "object"

4.28   to combinations of prime facts correspond same number of possibilities of truth and falsehood of n elementary propositions

4.441   to complex of signs F and T no object or complex of objects corresponds

4.466   to definite logical combination of signs corresponds definite logical combination of meanings

5.5542   we cannot set out a sign form without knowing whether anything corresponds to it

6.341   to different nets correspond different systems of world description

Create [erschaffen]

5.123   God cannot create world where p is true without creating world in which all consequents of p are true, or without creating all objects of p

Critique of Language [Sprachkritik]

4.0031   all philosophy is critique of language

Cube [Würfel]

5.5423   figure seen two ways as cube really two different derivative facts

-D-

Darwin, Charles

    4.1122 Darwin's theory not more philosophical than any other
            hypothesis of natural science

Death [Tod]

    6.431   in death world does not change but ceases

    6.4311 death not an event of life to be survived

    6.4312 eternal survival after death not assured

Declaration (statement) [Angabe]

    3.317   establishing values of propositional variable is the
            declaration of propositions whose common mark the
            variable is

    4.26   declaration of all true elementary propositions com-
            pletely describes world

    5.554   declaration of any special forms would be entirely
            arbitrary

Deduce [folgern]

    5.132   if p follows from q I can deduce p from q

    5.134   from an elementary proposition no other can be de-
            duced

Default [Ermanglung]

    5.156   only in default of certainty do we need probability

Defining [Definieren]

    5.42   possibility of crosswise defining of logical proto-
            signs of Frege and Russell shows that these are not
            proto-signs, and they designate no relationships

Definition [Definition]

    3.24   combination of symbols of complex in a simple symbol
            expressible by a definition

    3.26   name cannot be dismembered further through definition

    3.261   every defined sign signifies via the defining signs,
            as shown by definition; names cannot be taken to
            pieces by definition

36   Definition [Definition] continued

3.343   definitions are rules for translation of one language
into another

4.241   definition of a new sign written like an equation;
definition is a sign rule

5.451   what Frege says about introduction of signs by definitions holds also for introduction of proto-signs

5.452   definitions in words in Principia Mathematica require
justification which cannot be given

5.5302   Russell's definition of equality unsatisfactory

6.02   definition of number in terms of series

Definitive [definitiv]

Foreword: truth of thoughts communicated in Tractatus is
definitive

Degree [Grad]

5.155   that circumstances give such and such degree of
probability to occurrences of determined event is
unity of probability proposition

6.1271   it is remarkable that Frege appealed to degree of self-
evidence as criterion of logical proposition

Delimit [abgrenzen]

4.112   philosophy should sharply delimit thoughts otherwise
dull and turbid

Delimit [begrenzen]

5.5262   range allowed to construction of world by totality
of elementary propositions is what completely general
propositions delimit

Demonstrate [demonstrieren]

6.121   propositions of logic demonstrate logical properties
of propositions

Denial (negation) [Verneinung]

3.42   denial cannot introduce new elements

4.0621   that denial occurs in a proposition is not a characteristic of its sense

4.064   like affirmation, denial cannot give a proposition
sense, for this is what is denied

4.0641   denial is already related to logical locus determined
by proposition denied

5.2341   denial reverses sense of a proposition

Denial (negation) [Verneinung] continued

 5.254 operations, e.g. denial, can vanish

 5.44 denial is not material function

 5.451 denial introduced as fundamental logical concept

 5.512 what is common to all denying signs mirrors denial

 6.231 affirmation can be conceived as double denial

Deny (negate) [verneinen]

 4.0641 denial is already related to logical locus determined
by proposition denied; denying proposition determines
a logical locus other than that of proposition denied;
denying proposition determines a logical locus with
help of logical locus of proposition denied; that one
can again deny denied proposition shows that what is
denied is already a proposition

 5.44 ~~p does not treat denial as an object

 5.512 what denies in ~p is what is common to all signs denying p; this mirrors denial

Depend [abhängen]

 2.0211 propositions would depend on each other for truth if
there were no world

 3.315 class of propositions which are values of variable
proposition produced by changing a constituent to a
variable, depends on arbitrary agreement about parts
of proposition; class of propositions as values remains when all arbitrary signs are changed to variables, and this depends on no agreement, but no nature
of proposition

 5.231 operation will depend on formal properties of base and
resultant propositions, on internal similarity of
their forms

 5.25 only result of operation asserts, and this depends on
bases

 5.474 number of necessary fundamental operations depends
only on our notation

Dependence [Unselbständigkeit]

 2.0122 form of dependence a form of independence

Derivative Fact (fact, molecular fact, secondary fact) [Tatsache].
See also Case; Factually; Prime Fact: State of Affairs
(Our translation has no special claim. It is useful chiefly
to draw an important distinction between Tatsache and Sachverhalt. "Fact" may still be the best rendering, on an
analogy: the simplest propositions are elementary propositions, and the simplest facts are prime, or atomic, facts.

38   Derivative Fact (fact, molecular fact, secondary fact)
      [Tatsache] continued

          Wittgenstein does say that Tatsachen are composed of
          Sachverhalte, but this is no reason to suppose that it is
          a synthesis of like parts which makes a whole which is
          merely larger. Rather, there seems to be a functional
          relation between the two kinds of facts, and our arbi-
          trary rendering should serve to bring this out. $Fact_1$
          and $Fact_2$ might do as well (if understood to designate
          distinct kinds of facts) simply because all other trans-
          lations are imperfect and misleading. We deplore the
          barbaric sound of our phrase, but elegance would help
          little in an index.)

    1.1   totality of derivative facts is the world

    1.11   world is determined by the derivative facts, and
             by there being no others

    1.12   totality of derivative facts determines what is
             and what is not the case

    1.13   derivative facts in logical space are world

    1.2   world breaks up into derivative facts

    2.   derivative fact is the subsistence of prime facts

    2.0121   all possibilities are the derivative facts of
             logic

    2.034   structure of derivative facts consists of struc-
             ture of prime facts

    2.06   subsistence of prime fact is a positive deriva-
             tive fact, non-subsistence a negative

    2.1   we make images of derivative facts for ourselves

    2.141   image is a derivative fact

    2.16   derivative facts have something in common with
             imaged in order for latter to be an image

    3.   logical image of derivative facts is the thought

    3.14   propositional sign is a derivative fact

    3.142   only derivative facts express a sense

    3.143   propositional sign is a derivative fact, but
             ordinary form of expression conceals this

    4.016   hieroglyphic writing images derivative facts

    4.0312   logical constants do not stand as proxies for
             logic of derivative facts

    4.061   propositions have sense independent of derivative
             facts

Derivative Fact (fact, molecular fact, secondary fact)
    [Tarsache] continued

    4.063   derivative fact and black spot on white paper to ex-
             plain concept of truth

    4.122   we speak of properties of structure of derivative
             facts, and these are called "internal properties"

    4.1221   internal property of derivative facts a feature of
             derivative facts

    4.1272   "derivative fact" designates formal concept and is
             represented in ideography by a variable

    4.2211   even if each derivative fact consists of infinity of
             prime facts, there must be prime facts

    4.463   elbowroom left to derivative fact by proposition is
             determined by truth-conditions

    5.43   that from derivative fact p infinitely more follow is
             scarcely to be believed

    5.461   apparently unimportant derivative fact that logical
             pseudo-relations like v and ⊃ need brackets, in
             opposition to actual relations, is full of meaning

  * 5.5151   whether negative proposition is expressible by nega-
             tive derivative fact

    5.542   derivative fact co-ordinated with object by means of
             co-ordination of objects in "'p' says p"

    5.5423   a figure seen two ways as cube is two different deriv-
             ative facts

    6.111   if "true" and "false" designate properties, then the
             remarkable derivative fact appears that every pro-
             position possesses one of these properties

    6.113   derivative fact of self-evidence of logical proposi-
             tions contains whole philosophy of logic

    6.2321   propositions of mathematics can be seen to be correct
             without having to compare what they express with
             derivative facts

    6.43   willing may change limits of the world but not the
             derivative facts, or what can be expressed in
             language

    6.4321   derivative facts all belong to task, not to solution

Derivatively Factually. See Factually

Describe [beschreiben]

    2.0201   assertions about complexes analyzed into those about
             constituents and those which completely describe
             complexes

Description [Beschreibung] 41

4.023   proposition a description of a prime fact; the descrip-
        tion of an object describes it by external properties

* 4.5   characteristics of description of general form of propo-
        sition

5.02   index is always part of description of object to whose
        name we attach it

5.156   probability involves general description of proposi-
        tional form

5.4711 to supply essence of proposition means to give essence
        of all description, thus essence of world

5.472   description of most general form of proposition is
        description of one general proto-sign of logic

5.501   determination of values of a variable is a description
        of propositions for which variable stands; how this
        description takes place unessential; description is of
        three kinds

6.125   "true" logical propositions can receive description
        even in old logic

6. 341 Newtonian mechanics brings description of world to
        united form; description of white surface with black
        spots; possibly simpler descriptions; mechanics deter-
        mines a form of description of world by using few
        axioms

6.343   mechanics an attempt to construct all true proposi-
        tions needed for description of world

6.3432 description of world by mechanics is quite general

6.3611 description of temporal sequence of events possible
        only if we support ourselves on another process

Designate (signify) [bezeichnen]

3.24   that propositional element designates complex seen in
        indeterminateness of its propositions

3.261   every defined sign designates via defining signs; a
        proto-sign and a sign defined by proto-signs cannot
        designate in same way

3.321   different symbols can have sign in common but desig-
        nate in different ways

3.322   it cannot indicate common mark of two objects that we
        designate them with same sign but different ways of
        designating

3.323   in colloquial language it often happens that same
        word designates in different ways and so belongs to
        different symbols, or that two words which designate
        in different ways are outwardly applied in same way
        in proposition

42   Designate (signify) [bezeichnen] continued

    3.325   to avoid errors we must employ sign language which excludes them, by not applying same sign in different symbols and by not applying signs in same way which designate in different ways

    3.333   sign by itself designates nothing

    3.334   rules of logical syntax must be self-evident if one knows how every sign designates

    3.411   the proper name is what all symbols which designate object have in common

    3.344   what designates in symbol is what is common to all symbols by which it can be replaced according to rules of logical syntax

    4.063   to proposition without sense corresponds nothing, for it designates no thing whose properties are called false or true

    4.126   the name shows that it designates an object, the numerical sign that it designates a number, etc.

    4.127   the propositional variable designates formal concept, and its values designate objects which fall under that concept

    4.1272   such words as "complex," "derivative fact," etc., designate formal concepts and are represented by variables, not functions or classes

    4.243   impossible to understand two names without knowing wnether they designate same thing or different things

    5.42   possibility of crosswise definition of logical proto-signs of Frege and Russell snows these are not proto-signs, and they designate no relationships

    5.473   a possible sign must be able to designate

Designated (signified) [bezeichnet]

    4.012   sign a likeness of what is designated

    4.061   true and false not relations between signs and what is designated; we cannot say that "p" designates in true way what "~p" designates in false way

    4.442   Frege's assertion sign merely shows that user holds as true the propositions so designated

    5.476   our concern is not number of fundamental concepts to be designated, but expression of a rule

Designated [Bezeichnete]

    3.317   essential to determination of values of proposi-tional variable only that it be a description of

Designated [Bezeichnete] continued

> symbols and assert nothing about what is designated

Designating [bezeichnend]

5.4733   when "identical" occurs as sign of equality, the designating relation differs from possible adjectival use

5.5261   signs in generalized proposition stand independently in designating relation to world as in ungeneralized proposition

Designation (symbolization, signification) [Bezeichnung]

3.322   if we chose different manners of designating, what would become of what is common to designations?

4.0411   expressions which are inadequate for designation of generalization

5.02   designation which depends on arbitrary agreement could be handled by simple sign as well as complex

5.1311   method of designation can conceal relation between forms of propositions

Designation of Generality [Allgemeinheitsbezeichnung]

4.0411   difficulties in designation of generality using an index

5.522   two peculiarities of designation of generality

5.523   designation of generality occurs as an argument

6.1203   recognition of tautology in cases where designation of generality does not occur

Determinate [bestimmt]

4.466   to determinate logical union of signs corresponds union of their meanings

5.475   number of necessary fundamental operations rests only upon constructing system of signs having determinate number of dimensions--of determinate mathematical multiplicity

6.124   that certain combinations of symbols which essentially have determinate character are tautologies points to something about world

Determinateness [Bestimmtheit]

3.23   postulate of possibility of simple signs is postulate of determinateness of the sense

Determination [Bestimmung]

4.431   Frege's determination of sense for ~p not adequate

Determined (definite) [bestimmt] continued

4.442   number of truth-conditions determined by number of
propositions

5.11   if truth-grounds common to number of propositions are
truth-grounds of some determined proposition, truth of
this proposition follows from truth of those

5.155   that circumstances give such and such degree of probability to occurrence of determined event is unit of
probability proposition

5.526   one can completely describe world without co-ordinat-
ing any name with determined object

6.342   image can be completely described by a determined net
of determined fineness

6.3432   in world description by mechanics is never any discussion of determined material points, only of some
points or other

Differ [verschieden]

5.4733   when "identical" occurs as sign of equality, the designating relation differs from possible adjectival use

Difference [Verschiedenheit]

5.24   operation gives expression to differences between
forms

5.241   operation characterizes difference between forms

5.53   difference of objects is expressed by difference of
signs

Different [verschieden]

2.0233   two objects of same logical form are, apart from external properties, differentiated from one another in
that they are different

3.321   different symbols can have sign in common but designate
in different ways

3.322   it cannot indicate common mark of two objects that we
designate them with same sign but different ways of
designating

3.323   in colloquial language same word often designates in
different ways, so belongs to different symbols, or
two words which designate in different ways are out-
wardly applied in same way in proposition

3.325   to avoid errors we must employ sign language which excludes them, by not applying same sign in different
symbols and by not applying signs in same way which
designate in different ways

4.243   impossible to understand two names without knowing

Disagreement [Nichtübereinstimmung] continued

    4.4   proposition an expression of disagreement with truth-
            possibilities of elementary proposition

    4.42   number of possibilities of disagreement with truth-
            possibilities of elementary propositions

    4.43   means of expressing disagreement with truth-possibili-
            ties in schema

    4.431   disagreement with truth-possibilities of elementary
            propositions expresses certain truth-conditions of the
            proposition

Disclosed (inferred) [erschliessen]

    5.136   events of future cannot be disclosed through those
            of present

Disguise. See Clothe

Dismembered (analysed) [zergliedert]. See also Take Apart

    3.26   name cannot be dismembered through definitions

Display [weisen]

    2.172   image displays its form of imaging

Disputable [bestreitbar]

    4.113   philosophy limits disputable sphere of natural
            science

Dissolution [Auflösung]

    4.466   tautology and contradiction are limiting cases of
            combinations of signs, their dissolution

Distinguish [herausheben, hervorheben]

    2.02331 if a thing has properties no other has, one can dis-
            tinguish it directly; if a thing is not distinguished,
            one cannot distinguish it, or it would be distinguished

Distinguishing Mark [Abzeichen]

    4.43   agreement with truth-possibilities expressed by co-
            ordinating them with distinguishing mark T; its
            absence means disagreement

    4.44   sign arising from co-ordination of distinguishing mark
            is a propositional sign

Divide. See Break Up

Divided [zerlegen]

    2.0201   statement about complexes can be divided into state-
            ment about constituents and into propositions com-
            pletely describing complexes

48   Doctrine (theory) [Lehre]. See also Activity; Theory

     4.112   philosophy not a doctrine but an activity

     6.1224   logic is called doctrine of forms and inferences

     6.13   logic not a doctrine

Doubt [Zweifel]

     6.51   skepticism nonsensical if it would doubt where a
             question cannot be asked; doubt can only exist
             where something can be said

     6.521   after long doubt the sense of life, when finally
             clear, cannot be said

Dualism [Dualismus]

     4.128   no philosophical monism or dualism, because no
             pre-eminent numbers

Dynamical [dynamisch]

   *   4.04   dynamical models in Hertz' mechanics, and mathe-
             matical multiplicity

-E-

Effect [Wirkung]

     5.253   one operation can reverse effect of another

     5.46   with introduction of effect of all possible com-
             binations of brackets, nature of proper proto-
             signs becomes clear

Effects [Folgen]

     6.422   effects of an action irrelevant to ethics

Elbowroom (range, play, free play) [Spielraum]
     ("Range" has taken on a technical meaning in logistic which
     makes it an unwise choice here.)

     4.463   elbowroom left to the derivative facts through the
             proposition determined by the truth-conditions

     5.5262   elbowroom allowed to world's construction by all ele-
             mentary propositions is that which general proposi-
             tions delimit

Element [Element]

     2.13   elements of image correspond to objects

     2.131   elements of image stand as proxies for objects

Element [Element] continued   49

2.14   in the image elements are related in a definite way

2.15   that elements are related represents that entities are
          related; coherence of elements of image is its
          structure

2.151   form of imaging is possibility that the things are re-
          lated as the elements of the image are

2.1514   imaging relation is co-ordination of elements of image
          and entities

2.1515   co-ordinations are like feelers of elements touching
          actuality

3.14   in propositional sign its elements, the words, are re-
          lated in a definite manner

3.2   in propositions objects of thoughts correspond to
          elements of propositional sign

3.201   elements are simple signs

3.24   propositional element designating complex creates an
          indeterminateness in propositions in which it occurs

Elementary Proposition [Elementarsatz]

4.21   elementary proposition is simplest kind; asserts
          existence of a prime fact

4.211   no other elementary proposition can contradict an
          elementary proposition

4.22   elementary proposition consists of names

4.221   analysis of propositions must come finally to elemen-
          tary propositions

4.23   name occurs in proposition only in connection of the
          elementary proposition

4.24   elementary proposition is written as a function of
          names in form "fx," etc.

4.243   "a = a" or other deduced expressions are not elemen-
          tary propositions

4.25   if elementary proposition is true, a prime fact
          exists; if false, it does not

4.26   specification of all true elementary propositions
          completely describes world

4.28   possibilities of truth and falsehood of n elementary
          propositions correspond to combinations of prime
          facts

4.3   truth-possibilities of elementary propositions mean
          possibilities of existence and non-existence of prime
          facts

Elementary Proposition [Elementarsatz] continued

5.31   truth-table schemata are significant even if p,q, etc., are not elementary propositions

5.32   truth-functions are results of successive application of finite number of truth-operations to elementary propositions

5.41   all results of truth-operations on same truth-function of elementary propositions are identical

5.47   all logical operations are contained in elementary proposition

5.5   truth-functions result from application of operation (----T) (ξ.....) to elementary propositions

5.524   if elementary propositions are given with sign of generality, then all elementary propositions are given

5.5262   elbowroom allowed to world's construction by totality of elementary propositions is what the completely generalized propositions delimit; if an elementary proposition is true, then one more elementary proposition is true

5.55   question regarding all possible forms of elementary propositions to be answered a priori; the elementary proposition consists of names, but we cannot give its composition

5.555   we have concept of elementary proposition apart from its special logical form

5.556   no hierarchy of forms of elementary propositions

5.5561   limit of empirical reality appears in totality of elementary propositions

5.5562   elementary propositions must be known to exist by everyone understanding them in their unanalyzed form

5.557   application of logic determines which elementary propositions there are

5.5571   if elementary propositions cannot be given a priori, it is nonsense to try to give them

6.001   every proposition the result of successive applications of $N'(\xi)$ to elementary propositions

6.124   logical propositions presuppose that elementary propositions have sense

6.3751   logical product of two elementary propositions cannot be a tautology or a contradiction

Elucidate [erläutern]

6.54   Wittgenstein's propositions elucidate because he who understands recognizes them as nonsensical in the end

Equality of Numbers. See Numerical Equality   53

Equation [Gleichung]

* 4.241   how equation for substitution of signs is written

  6.2   propositions of mathematics are equations, hence
           illusory propositions

  6.22   equations show in mathematics what tautologies show
           in logic about logic of world

  6.232   in equation, the question is unnecessary for showing
           that expressions combined by sign of equality have
           same meaning

  6.2323   equation marks standpoint for considering two expres-
           sions

  6.2341   essential of mathematical method is working with
           equations

  6.24   method by which mathematics arrives at equations is
           that of substitution; equations express the replace-
           ment of two expressions

Equivalent [äquivalent]

  5.232   internal relation which orders series is equivalent to
           operation by which one member arises from another

  5.2523   concept of successive application of operation equiva-
           lent to concept "and so forth"

  5.47321 signs which serve one purpose are logically equiva-
           lent

Error [Irrtum]. See also Mistake

  3.325   to avoid errors we need sign-language excluding them,
           hence following logical syntax

  3.331   Russell's error in drawing up sign rules lies in
           speaking of what is meant by his signs

Essence (nature) [Wesen]

  3.1431   essence of propositional sign clear when we think of
           it as made up of spatial objects

* 3.342   limited arbitrary character resulting from essence of
           notation

  3.3421   possibility of every thing reveals part of essence of
           world

  4.016   to know essence of proposition, consider hieroglyphics;
           alphabet came from hieroglyphics without loss of
           essence of imaging

  4.027   it is in essence of proposition to impart a new sense

  5.471   general form of proposition is essence of proposition

Essentially [wesentlich] continued   55

    4.112   a philosophical work consists essentially in elucida-
             tions

    6.124   certain combinations of symbols with essentially a
             definite character are tautologies; in logic the nature
             of an essentially necessary sign itself asserts

    6.127   no essentially fundamental laws among propositions of
             logic

Establish (fix) [festlegen]

    5.514   if notation is established, there is a rule according to
             which all propositions affirming p are formed

Establish (state) [feststellen]

    4.003   we cannot answer most philosophical questions at all,
             but only establish their nonsensicality

Eternal [ewig]

    6.4312   eternal life just as much a riddle as present one

Eternity [Ewigkeit]

    6.4311   if eternity is timelessness, then he lives eternally
             who lives in the present

Ethical [ethisch]

    6.422   ethical reward and punishment must lie in an action it-
             self

    6.423   of will as bearer of the ethical nothing can be spoken

Ethics [Ethik]

    6.42   no propositions of ethics

    6.421   ethics cannot be enunciated; is transcendental; and
             esthetics are one

    6.422   ethics has nothing to do with punishment and reward in
             ordinary sense

Event [Ereignis]

    5.1361   events of future cannot be inferred from those of present

    5.153   event occurs or does not occur; no middle course

    5.154   two events are established by experiment to be indepen-
             dent of circumstances which I do not know better

    5.452   introduction of new device in logical symbolism must
             always be consequential event

    6.3611   description of temporal or spatial sequence of events is
             possible only if we support ourselves on another process

56   Event [Ereignis] continued

> 6.422   consequences of an ethical action will not be events
>
> 6.4311 death is not an event of life

Everything. See All

Evidence [Einleuchten]

> 5.1363 if from fact that proposition is evident to us it does
> not follow that it is true, then evidence is no justi-
> fication for belief in its truth

Evil [böse]

> 6.43   evil willing could only change world's limits, not
> derivative facts

Exhibit [aufweisen]. See also Display

> 4.121   proposition exhibits logical form of actuality

Exist [existieren]. See also Subsist

> 3.032   co-ordinates of point which does not exist cannot be
> given
>
> 3.24   a proposition speaking of a complex that does not exist
> is false, not nonsensical
>
> 3.323   in colloquial language "to exist" appears as intransi-
> tive verb like "to go"

Existence [Existenz]. See also Non-subsistence; Subsistence
("Existence," for Wittgenstein, often implies a construct of
some sort, a logical synthesis.)

> 3.323   word "is" as an expression of existence
>
> 3.4   existence of a locus in logical space assured by
> existence of the constituents
>
> 3.411   geometrical and logical locus agree in that each is
> possibility of an existence
>
> 4.1274 question about existence of a formal concept is
> nonsense
>
> 5.5151 positive proposition must presuppose existence of
> negative proposition, and conversely

Expedient [Behelf]. See also Snags

> 4.242   expressions of form "a = b" are expedients in presenta-
> tion
>
> 5.452   introduction of new expedient in logic must always be
> clarified

Experience [Erfahrung]

> 5.552   "experience" that we need to understand logic is that

Experience [Erfahrung] continued

> something is, but that is no experience; logic pre-
> cedes every experience

5.553   whether experience is needed to decide that simple re-
        lations exist between different numbers of things

5.634   no part of experience is also a priori

6.1222 logical propositions neither refuted nor established
        by experience

6.363   induction a process of assuming simplest law harmo-
        nizing with experience

Experiment [Experiment]

6.2331 calculation is not an experiment

Experiment [Versuch]

5.154   experiment with urn and black and white balls es-
        tablishes that two events are independent of certain
        circumstances

Experimentally. See On Approval

Explain [erklären]. See Clarify

Explain [verständigen]. See Interpret

Explanation. See Clarification

Exponent [Exponent]

6.021   a number is the exponent of an operation

Express [ausdrücken]

3.1   thought expresses itself through senses in proposition

3.13   possibility of expressing sense contained in proposi-
        tion

3.142   derivative facts express a sense

3.1431 spatial relations can express sense of proposition

3.2   proposition can express correspondence between objects
        and elements of propositional sign

3.24   definition can express combination of symbols in a
        simple symbol

3.251   proposition expresses what it expresses in a definite
        way

3.34   essential features of proposition are those which ex-
        press its sense

3.341   essential in proposition is what is common to all
        propositions which can express same sense

58   Express [ausdrücken]   continued

* 3.3441   how to express what is common to all notations for
            truth-functions

  4.013   irregularities in notation also image what they are
            to express

  4.0411   impossible to express what is expressed by, e.g.,
            (x) . fx

  4.121   what expresses itself in language cannot be expressed
            by language

  4.124   internal properties of possible state of affairs ex-
            press themselves by internal property of proposition
            presenting that state of affairs

  4.125   internal relation between possible states of affairs
            expresses itself by internal relation between proposi-
            tions presenting them

  4.1272   word "object" rightly expressed in ideography by
            variable name

  4.1273   what is needed to express "b is a successor of a";
            general member of formal series is expressed by varia-
            ble; way Frege and Russell expressed general properties
            is false

* 4.241   identity of meaning as expressed by sign " = "

  4.431   expression of agreement with truth-possibilities of
            elementary propositions expresses truth-conditions of
            proposition

  5.131   if truth of one proposition follows from truth of
            others, this expresses itself in relations in which
            forms of these propositions stand to one another

  5.31   propositional sign expresses truth-function of ele-
            mentary proposition

  5.503   means for construction of propositions out of operation
            is easy to express

* 5.5151   question raised of expressing negative proposition
            through negative derivative fact

  5.5301   sign of sameness needed to express that only a has a
            certain relation to a

* 6.1203   brackets used to express truth-combinations

  6.124   in logic it is not we who express what we want by
            means of signs

  6.21   propositions of mathematics express no thoughts

  6.2321   what propositions of mathematics express need not be
            compared to derivative facts for correctness

Express [ausdrücken] continued

    6.24   equations express replacement of two expressions

    6.42   propositions can express nothing higher

Expressed [ausgedrückt]

* Foreword: reader who understands thoughts expressed in
            Tractatus

    3.12   sign through which thought is expressed is proposi-
            tional sign

    4.002   every sense can be expressed in language

    4.1216   that anything falls under formal concept as its object
            cannot be expressed through a proposition

* 4.43   how agreement with truth-possibilities can be ex-
            pressed

    4.5   in general form of propositions, propositions of one
            sign-language are so described that every possible
            sense can be expressed by a symbol and every symbol
            can express a sense

    5.242   that same operation which makes q from p, makes r
            from q, etc., can only be expressed by fact that p,q,
            r are variables giving general expression to certain
            formal relations

    5.525   certainty, possibility, impossibility of some state of
            affairs is not expressed by proposition, but rather by
            expression's being a tautology, sense-bearing proposi-
            tion, or contradiction

    5.53   sameness of objects is expressed by sameness of signs

* 5.535   Axiom of Infinity expressed in language

    5.5352   "there are no things" is wrongly expressed by Russell

    6.1264   modus ponens cannot be expressed by a proposition

    6.43   things expressed in language not changed by good and
            bad willing

Expression [Ausdruck]

    Foreword: Tractatus draws limit to expression of thoughts;
             value of book consists in its expression of thoughts

    3.143   of propositional sign customary form of expression
            conceals factual character of proposition

    3.262   what cannot be given expression in sign is shown by
            application

    3.31   part of proposition which characterizes its sense

Expression [Ausdruck] continued   61

External [extern]

Factually (derivatively factually, in fact, actually) [tatsächlich]   63
  continued
  is not wrong here, though it does blur Wittgenstein's meaning
  a little. In truth the word shades over into a very casual
  adverbial expression such as "indeed" or "certainly."

  5.452   definitions in words in Principia Mathematica are
           factually not allowed

  5.5563   propositions of ordinary language are factually in
           order

  6.36111 right and left hands are factually congruent

False [falsch]. See also True; True or False; Truth
  (We do not give the many dozens of references to the text where
  the expression "false" or "F" is used as an arbitrary designation of any given proposition).

  2.17   image must have in common with actuality imaging rela-
           tion to image actuality rightly or falsely

  2.173   image stands for its object from without, so stands
           for it rightly or falsely

  2.18   image must have in common with actuality the logical
           form to image actuality at all, rightly or falsely

  3.24   proposition which speaks of complex, if this does not
           exist, is simply false, not nonsensical

  4.003   most propositions and questions about philosophical
           things are not false but nonsense

  4.061   to say "not-p designates in false way what p desig-
           nates in true way" is not to observe that the propo-
           sition has sense independent of derivative facts

  4.062   false propositions so intended are indistinguishable
           from true propositions

  4.063   to be able to call p true (or false) I must first know
           under what circumstances I call p true

  4.1273   way Frege and Russell express certain general proposi-
           tions is false and contains vicious circle

  4.26   world completely described by specification of all
           elementary propositions plus specification, which are
           true and which false

  4.431   Frege's explanation of the truth-concept is false

  5.5351   hypothesis for non-proposition as argument becomes not
           false, but nonsensical

  6.111   theories which make proposition of logic appear to
           have content are always false; "false" does not
           designate a property like natural properties

Finite [endlich]

    5.32   truth-functions are results of successive application of finite number of truth-operations to elementary propositions

Fixed [fest]

    2.023   fixed form of actual or imagined world must consist of objects

    2.026   only if there are objects can there be a fixed form of world

Fixed [das Feste]

    2.027   the fixed, subsistent, and object are one

    2.0271   the object is the fixed, the subsistent

Fixed [festgesetzt]

    3.316   which values the propositional variable can assume are fixed

    4.442   if series of truth-possibilities in schema is fixed by rule of combination, then last column is expression of truth-conditions

Fixed [fixiert]

    4.023   actuality must be fixed by proposition with respect to yes or no

Fixing [Festsetzung]

    3.316   fixing of values is the variable

    3.317   fixing of these values is the declaration of propositions whose common mark is the variable; is a description of these propositions; will deal only with symbols, not their meaning; only a description of symbols, not the designated

    5.501   fixing of values of a variable is description of the propositions for which variable stands

Follow [folgen]

    4.1211   if one proposition follows from another, this is shown by their structure

    5.11   if truth-grounds common to number of propositions are truth-grounds of some determined proposition, truth of latter follows from truth of former

    5.12   truth of p follows from that of q if truth-grounds of latter are truth-grounds of former

    5.121   truth-grounds of one proposition are contained in those of another, and p follows from q

Form [Form] continued   67

2.0233 two objects of same logical form are only differenti-
        ated in that they are different

2.025   object is form

2.0251 space, time, and color are forms of objects

2.026   fixed form of world depends upon objects

2.033   form of the objects is possibility of the structure
        of the prime facts

2.171   image can image every actuality whose form it has

2.18   logical form necessary in every image, true or false

2.181   logical form of image defines logical image

3.13   what proposition contains is the form of its sense

3.31   an expression marks a form and a content

3.311   expression presupposes forms of all propositions in
        which it can occur

3.312   expression is represented by general form of proposi-
        tions it characterizes

* 3.315 logical form and what corresponds to it

3.327   sign and logical syntactic application determine
        logical form

3.333   in F(F(fx)) the two functions have different forms

4.002   from external form of clothes no inference to form
        of thought they clothe

4.0031 apparent logical form of proposition need not be
        actual form

4.012   proposition of form aRb perceived as image

4.063   form of black spot on white paper described by net-
        work

4.12   propositions cannot represent logical form; we would
        need to put ourselves outside logic

4.121   propositions mirror logical form; proposition shows
        and exhibits logical form of actuality

4.1241 one cannot distinguish forms by means of properties

4.1271 every variable represents a constant form which all its
        values possess

4.1273 general term of formal series determined by giving
        first term and general form of operation

4.128   logical forms are anumerical

Form [Form] continued   69

5.55   question of all possible form of elementary propo-
          sitions

5.554   statement of special forms arbitrary

5.5542   we cannot set out a sign form and not know whether
          anything corresponds to it

5.555   we have concept of elementary proposition apart from
          its special logical form; invention of logical forms
          must be dealt with through that which makes it possible
          to invent them

5.556   no hierarchy of forms of elementary propositions

5.5562   if we know on logical grounds that there must be
          elementary propositions, this must be known from
          propositions in their unanalyzed form

5.6331   field of sight has not a form which includes eye

6.1201   that propositions bound up in certain form give tau-
          tology shows that they possess certain properties of
          structure

* 6.1203 form ~ ξ, etc., as written in bracket notation

6.1224   logic is called theory of forms and of inferences

6.1264   in logic every proposition is the form of a proof

6.23   logical form of equal expressions

6.32   law of causality is form of a law

6.321   form of law of causality in physics a class name

6.33   possibility of logical form known a priori

6.341   Newtonian mechanics brings description of universe
          to unified form; arbitrary form of mesh of network--
          triangular, square, etc.; unified; mechanics determines
          form of world-description

6.342   network of a given form can describe world, but asserts
          nothing about image

* 6.35   nothing can be said by geometry about factual form and
          position of spots in our image

* 6.422   ethical law having form of "Thou shalt . . ."

Form [bilden]
          (In a few places, bilden seems to mean not "to image" but "to
          form" - however much both these two meanings might be related
          to the shaping of clay or the like into a recognizable figure.)

2.021   objects form substance of world

2.0231   configuration of objects forms material properties
          of world

5.4733   Frege says every legitimately constructed proposition
         must have a sense

5.521   Frege's and Russell's introduction of generality in
         combination with logical product creates difficulties

6.1271   objection to Frege's appeal to self-evidence as cri-
         terion for fundamental laws of logic

6.232   Frege claims that "1 + 1 + 1 + 1" and "(1 + 1) and (1 + 1)"
         have same meaning, but different senses

Function [Funktion]. See also Truth-function

3.318   proposition is conceived as a function of expressions
         contained in it

3.333   function cannot be own argument, since functional
         sign already contains proto-image of its own argument

4.126   formal concepts cannot be represented by a function;
         their marks, the formal properties, are not expressed
         by functions

4.1272   "function," "number," etc., signify formal concepts
         and are not represented by functions

4.12721 one cannot introduce concept of function and also
         special functions as fundamental concepts

4.24   elementary propositions written as function of names
         in form "fx," etc.

5.02   to mistake arguments of functions for indices of names
         is easy; Frege erred here

5.2341   sense of truth-function of p is function of sense of p

5.25   operation and function must not be confused

5.251   a function cannot be its own argument

5.44   truth-functions are not material functions

5.47   where argument and function exist all logical constants
         exist

* 5.501   giving a function fx as a kind of description

* 5.52   fx and values of x

5.5301   in "(x):fx.⊃.x = a," only a satisfies function f

Fundamental [grundlegend]

4.411   elementary propositions are fundamental to understanding
         of other propositions

Fundamental Concept [Grundbegriff]

4.12721 formal concept and what falls under it cannot both be
         introduced as fundamental concepts

74   Fundamental Concept [Grundbegriff] continued

5.451   fundamental concepts are independent of one another

5.476   number of fundamental concepts specified through expression of a rule

Fundamental Law [Grundgesetz]

5.452   fundamental laws in words in Principia Mathematica are not allowed

6.127   no propositions of logic are in essence fundamental laws

6.1271   number of fundamental laws of logic is arbitrary

Fundamental Operation [Grundoperation]

5.42   that infinite number of propositions of logic (of mathematics) follow from half dozen "fundamental propositions" is scarcely to be believed

Fundamental Thought [Grundgedanke]

4.0312   Wittgenstein's fundamental thought is that logical constants do not represent

Future [Zukunft]

5.1361   events of future cannot be proved from those of present

5.1362   freedom of will consists in this, that future actions cannot be known now

-G-

Gather. See Extract

General (universal) [allgemein]

3.312   expression represented by general form of propositions it characterizes

3.315   class of propositions which are values of variable proposition produced by changing a constituent to a variable, depends in general on arbitrary agreement about parts of proposition

3.341   in general the essential in symbol is what symbols must have in common to fulfill same purpose

3.3441   that all notations for truth-functions can be replaced by notations of ~p and pvq indicates way special possible notation can give us general information

4.0141   inner similarity of symphony, score, etc., consists in general rule by which musician can read symphony out of score, etc.

General (universal) [allgemein] continued

    4.411   understanding of general propositions depends palpably upon understanding of elementary propositions

    4.5   general form of proposition is: such and such is so

    4.53   general propositional form is a variable

    5.156   probability involves a general description of propositional form

    5.242   that same operation which makes q from p, makes r from q, etc., can only be expressed by fact that p, q, r are variables giving general expression to certain formal relations

  * 5.2522   notation for general member of formal series explained

    5.454   in logic cannot be a more general and a more special

    5.46   proper general proto-signs are not p or q, etc., but the most general form of their combinations

    5.47   the one logical constant is the general form of proposition

    5.471   the general form of proposition is essence of proposition

    5.472   description of most general form of proposition is description of one general proto-sign of logic

    5.5262   truth or falsehood of every proposition alters something in general structure of world; range allowed to construction of world is what completely general propositions delimit

    5.54   in general propositional form proposition occurs in proposition only as basis of truth-operation

    6.1231   symptom of logical propositions is not their general validity; to be general is only to be accidentally valid for all things

    6.3432   description of world through mechanics is general

General Form [allgemeine Form]. See also Form; Special Form

  * 6.   general form of truth-function and proposition stated notationally

    6.002   general form of proposition also gives general form for changing one proposition to another

    6.01   general form of transition from one proposition to another stated notationally

    6.022   concept of number is general form of number; concept of equality of numbers is general form of all special equalities of numbers

  * 6.03   general form of number stated notationally

76   General Member (general term) [allgemeines Glied]

    4.1273   general member needed for expression of general proposition "b is a successor of a"; can only be expressed by a variable; can be determined by giving first member and general form of operation generating next member

General Proposition [allgemeiner Satz]

    4.1273   to express general proposition "b is successor of a" we need an expression for general terms of formal series

General Validity [Allgemeingültigkeit]

    6.1232   logical general validity, as opposed to accidental general validity, must be essential

Generality (universality) [Allgemeinheit]. See also Designation of Generality

    3.24   notation for generality contains a proto-image

    5.1311   method of designating may conceal generality in symbol

    5.521   Frege and Russell introduced generality with logical product and sum

    6.031   generality in mathematics is not accidental

Generalization [Verallgemeinerung]

    4.52   in a sense all propositions are generalizations of elementary propositions

    5.156   probability is a generalization

Generalized [verallgemeinert]

   * 4.0411   problem of showing what is generalized by general signs

    5.526   one can completely describe the world through fully generalized propositions

    5.5261   completely generalized proposition is composite

    6.1231   a generalized proposition can be tautologous

Generic Name [Gattungsname]

    6.321   "law of causality" a generic name

Geometrical [geometrisch]

    3.411   geometrical and logical loci are each the possibility of an existence

   * 6.35   spots in image geometrical; network is purely geometrical

Geometry [Geometrie]

    3.032   in geometry no figure can be presented which contradicts laws of space

Geometry [Geometrie] continued

    3.0321   laws of geometry could not be contradicted by a prime
                  fact

* 6.35   geometry can say nothing about factual form and posi-
                  tion of spots in image

Glove [Handschuh]

    6.36111 right-hand glove can be put on left hand if turned
                  round in 4-dimensional space

God [Gott]

    3.031   God could create everything except what was contrary
                  to laws of logic

    5.123   if a god creates world in which certain propositions
                  are true, he also creates thereby a world in which
                  all consequent propositions are true

    6.342   God does not reveal Himself in the world

    6.372   ancients stopped short at God and fate

Good [das Gute]

    4.003   whether good is more or less identical than the
                  beautiful is a nonsensical question

    6.43   good or evil willing, if it changes world, changes
                  only its limits, not its derivative facts

Gradation [Gradation]

    4.464   certain, possible, impossible are gradations in prob-
                  ability theory

Grammar [Grammatik]

    3.325   need for language obeying rules of logical grammar

Gramophone Record. See Phonograph Record

Green [grün]

    3.323   in "Green is green" first and last words have not
                  merely different meanings; rather they are different
                  symbols

Ground [Grund]

* 4.0412   ground for inadequacy of idealist's spatial spectacles

* 4.122   grounds for confusion between internal and external
                  relations

    4.126   ground for confusion of formal concepts with proper
                  concepts

    5.5562   knowledge of elementary propositions on logical grounds
                  open to all who understand propositions in unanalyzed
                  form

-H-

Hierarchy [Hierarchie]

    5.556   no hierarchy of forms of elementary propositions

    5.5561   of forms of elementary proposition are and must be independent of reality

Hieroglyphic Writing [Hieroglyphenschrift]

    4.016   to understand essence of the proposition we think of hieroglyphic writing, which images the derivative facts it describes

Higher [Höheres]

    6.42   propositions can express nothing higher

    6.432   how world is, is completely indifferent for what is higher

How [Wie]

    5.552   logic is before the "how," not before the "what"

    6.41   in world all is how it is and happens how it happens

    6.432   how world is, is completely indifferent for what is higher

    6.44   the mystical is not how the world is, but that it is

Human [menschlich]

    4.002   colloquial language is part of human organism and not less complicated; it is humanly impossible to extract immediately the logic of language

Hypothesis [Hypothese]

    4.1122 Darwinian theory no more philosophical than any other hypothesis

    5.5351 nonsense to place (p⊃p) as hypothesis before proposition to ensure form of argument, because hypothesis for a non-proposition as argument is nonsensical, not false

    6.36311 it is a hypothesis that sun will rise tomorrow

Hypothetically [hypothetisch]

    5.154   in experiment with urn and white and black balls, all known circumstances including natural laws hypothetically assumed give to occurrence of one event no more probability than to occurrence of other

-I-

I [Ich]

    5.63   I am my world (the microcosm)

Ideography (concept-writing, logical symbolism) [Begriffsschrift]

    3.325   ideography of Frege and Russell obeys rules of logical
               grammar but does not exclude all errors

    4.1272   when term "object," thing," etc., rightly used in ide-
               ography, it is expressed by variable name; formal con-
               cepts presented in ideography by variables

    4.1273   to express in ideography the general proposition "b is
               a successor of a" is needed an expression for general
               term of formal series

    4.431   truth-conditions constitute explanation of signs in
               Frege's ideography

    5.533   identity sign not essential constituent of ideography

  * 5.534   some illusory propositions that cannot be written in
               correct ideography

Illusion [Täuschung]

    6.371   notion that natural laws are clarifications of natural
               phenomena the illusion at basis of modern Weltan-
               schauung

Illusory Concept (pseudo-concept) [Scheinbegriff]

    4.1272   variable name "x" is proper sign of the illusory con-
               cept "object"

Illusory Proposition (pseudo-proposition) [Scheinsatz]

    4.1272   illusory propositions result from use of "object" etc.,
               as proper concepts

    5.534   illusory propositions like "a = a" cannot be written
               in correct ideography

    5.535   all problems connected with illusory propositions dis-
               appear in correct ideography

    6.2   propositions of mathematics are illusory propositions

Illusory Relation (pseudo-relation) [Scheinbeziehung]

    5.461   that logical illusory relations like v and ⊃ need
               brackets, in opposition to actual relations, is full of
               meaning

Image (picture) [Bild]. See also Proto-Image
    (Despite virtually universal acceptance of "picture," we think
    "image" a better word here simply because Wittgenstein's chief
    account of "proposition" as a kind of image, is of 3-dimension-
    al things - tables, chairs, etc. One thinks of a picture as
    being complete and of predetermined extent, whereas an image
    is informal. The dictionaries do not, as a rule, especially
    favor either word over the other one as the correct translation.)

    2.0212   image of world impossible without substance

    2.1   we make images of derivative facts for ourselves

Index to Terms

Image (picture) [Bild]. <u>See</u> <u>also</u> Proto-Image continued

2.202 image represents possible state of affairs in logical space

2.203 image contains possibility of state of affairs

2.21 image is true or false by agreeing with actuality or not

2.22 image represents what it represents, independently of the truth

2.221 image represents its sense

2.223 image is compared with actuality to discover truth

2.224 truth is not given in the image

2.225 no image is a priori true

3. logical image of derivative fact is thought

3.001 "prime fact is thinkable" means it can be imaged

3.01 totality of true thoughts is image of the world

3.42 logical scaffolding around image determines logical space

4.01 proposition is image of actuality

4.011 proposition, musical score, etc., are images of what they represent, even though not apparently so

4.012 proposition of form aRb perceived as an image

4.013 irregularities in image can image what they should express

4.021 proposition an image of actuality, for I know state of affairs presented by it

4.03 proposition is logical image of state of affairs; proposition can assert only by being an image

4.0311 proposition is put together as a living image

4.032 proposition is image only insofar as it is logically articulated

4.06 propositions are true or false only as they are images of actuality

4.063 image to explain concept of truth: black spot on white paper

4.462 tautology and contradiction are not images of actuality

4.463 image is like solid body limiting movement of others; or like empty space

5.156 proposition can be incomplete image of certain state of affairs, but is always <u>a</u> complete image

Imaging (picturing) [das Abbilden, Abbildung]. See also Form of
    Imaging

    4.015   possibility of all imagery of our means of expression
                rests on logic of imaging

    4.016   alphabet came from hieroglyphics without the essential
                in imaging being lost

    4.041   one cannot get outside mathematical multiplicity of
                image and imaged in imaging

Imaging (picturing) [abbildend]

    2.1513   imaging relation belongs to image

    2.1514   imaging relation consists of co-ordinations of elements
                of images and things

Immortality [Unsterblichkeit]

    6.4312   temporal immortality of soul not guaranteed nor does
                it solve riddle of life in space and time

Impart (communicate) [mitteilen]

    4.027   essential to propositions they can impart a new sense

    4.03   a proposition imparts a new sense with old words; a
                proposition imparts a state of affairs

Impossibility [Unmöglichkeit]

    5.525   impossibility of state of affairs expressed by contra-
                diction

    6.375   there is only logical impossibility

Impossible [unmöglich]

    2.0122   impossible for words to occur both alone and in the
                proposition

    2.0212   impossible to sketch image of substanceless world

    2.02331   objects with all same properties impossible to distinguish

    4.002   humanly impossible to gather immediately the logic of
                language

    4.243   impossible to know meanings of two synonymous words and
                not know that they are synonymous

    4.464   truth of contradiction is impossible; certain, possible,
                and impossible indicate probability-theory gradations

    5.5422   impossible to judge a nonsense

    6.3751   logically impossible for two colors to be in same place
                in visual field

Indefiniteness [Unbestimmtheit]

    3.24   indefiniteness shows that a propositional element
                signifies a complex

86   Independence [Selbständigkeit]

    2.0122 form of independence is a form of unity and dependence

  Independent [unabhängig]

    2.024 substance independent of what is the case

    2.061 prime facts independent of each other

    2.22 image represents what it represents, independently of its truth or falsehood

    4.061 the proposition has a sense independent of derivative facts

    5.152 propositions with no truth-arguments in common are called independent

    5.154 what is confirmed by experiment in probability is that occurrence of two events is independent of circumstances with which I have no closer acquaintance

    5.451 if logic has fundamental concepts, these must be independent of one another

    5.5261 signs in generalized proposition stand independently in designating relation to world as in ungeneralized proposition

    5.5561 hierarchies must be independent of reality

    6.373 world is independent of my will

  Independently [selbständig]

    3.261 signs independently having meaning cannot be taken to pieces by definition

  Index [Index]

    5.02 index is part of description of the object; index and argument must not be confused

  Individuals (Eng.)

    5.553 Russell asserts relations between different numbers of individuals

  Induction [Induktion]

    6.31 law of induction not a logical law; not a priori

    6.363 process of induction is that of assuming simplest law harmonizing with nature

  Inenunciable (inexpressible) [Unaussprechliches]. See also Enunciate

    6.522 the mystical is the inenunciable

  Infer (conclude) [schliessen]

    2.062 cannot infer subsistence of one prime fact from another

Infer (conclude) [schliessen] continued

4.002   cannot infer form of clothed thought from form of
         clothes

5.132   if p follows from q, I can infer p from q

5.633   from nothing in visual field can we infer seeing eye

6.211   we infer from one non-mathematical proposition to
         another by means of a mathematical proposition

Inference [Folgern]

5.133   all inference takes place a priori

Inference [Schliessen]

6.1224   logic has been called theory of forms and inference

Inference [Schluss]

5.132   method of inference must be understood from two propo-
         sitions alone

5.136   no causal nexus justifies inference from one state of
         affairs to a different one

5.1362   we could only know future actions if causality were an
         inner necessity like logical inference

Infinite [unendlich]. See also Limitless

2.0131   spatial object must lie in infinite space

4.2211   if world is infinitely complex, so that every deriva-
         tive fact consists of infinite number of prime facts
         and every prime fact of infinite number of objects,
         still there must be objects and prime facts

4.463   tautology leaves to actuality the whole infinite logi-
         cal space

5.43   that infinite number of propositions of logic (of
         mathematics) follows from half dozen "fundamental propo-
         sitions" is scarcely to be believed

6.4311   if by eternity is understood not infinite temporal
         duration but timelessness, he lives eternally who lives
         in the present

Infinitely [unendlich]

5.511   logic can use special snags only because these are
         connected by an infinitely fine network to great
         mirror

5.535   Axiom of Infinity is expressed in language by saying
         that there are infinitely many names with different
         meanings

Information [Aufschluss]

3.3421   the possibility of every single thing gives us infor-
         mation about essence of world

Internal [intern] continued

    5.231   operation will depend on formal properties of base
              and resultant propositions, on internal similarity
              of their forms

    5.232   internal relation ordering a series equivalent to an
              operation

Interpret (explain) [verständigen]

    4.026   by means of propositions, we interpret ourselves

Introduction [Einführung]

    4.411   introduction of elementary propositions fundamental
              for comprehension of other propositions

    5.451   what Frege has said about introduction of signs by
              definition holds too for introduction of proto-signs

    5.452   introduction of new device in symbolism of logic must
              always be consequential event

Intuition [Anschauung]. See also Insights

    6.233   language answers question whether intuition is needed
              for solution of mathematical problems

    6.2331   calculation brings about intuition needed for solution
              of mathematical problems

    6.45   intuition of world sub specie aeterni an intuition of
              it as limited whole

Intuitive [anschaulich]

  * 6.1203   intuitive method for recognizing tautologies given

Investigation [Erforschung]. See also Study

    6.3   investigation of logic means investigation of all con-
              formity to law

Investigations [Untersuchungen]

    4.1121   philosophers studying thought processes got entangled
              in inessential psychological investigations

Irregularities [Unregelmässigkeiten]

    4.013   irregularities also image what they are to express,
              only in another way

-J-

Jointed [gegliedert]. See also Articulated

    4.032   proposition an image of a state of affairs only inso-
              far as it is logically jointed

Language [Sprache] continued

4.002   man possesses capacity for constructing languages; every sense can be expressed; language clothes the thought

4.003   most questions and propositions of philosophers result from not understanding logic of language

4.014   language related to world in same imaging internal relation as one that holds between musical score, musical thought, soundwaves

4.0141   rule of translation projects language of musical score into language of phonograph record

* 4.025   process of translating one language into another

4.1121   Wittgenstein's study of sign-language like that of thought processes

4.121   what mirrors itself in language latter cannot represent; what expresses itself in language we cannot express by it

4.1213   if sign language is right, logical conception seems right

4.125   possible relations between states of affairs expressed in languages between propositions representing them

5.4731   self-evidence can only be done away with if logic of language itself prevents each logical mistake

* 5.535   Axiom of Infinity as expressed in language

5.5563   propositions of colloquial language in order just as they are

5.6   limits of my language mean limits of my world

5.62   limits of language that I understand are also the world's limits

6.12   logical properties of language shown in tautological character of logical propositions

6.233   provides intuition for solution of mathematical problems

6.43   things expressible in language not alterable by writing

Law [Gesetz]. See also Conformity to Law; Rule

3.031   God cannot create what is contrary to logical laws

3.032   nothing contradicting laws of space can be presented in geometry

3.0321   laws of physics can be contradicted by a prime fact; of geometry cannot be contradicted by a prime fact presented in space

Life [Leben]

    5.621   life and the world are one

    6.211   in life, we never use a mathematical proposition

    6.4311   death not an event of life; life is endless just as visual field is without limit

    6.4312   solution of riddle of life lies outside space and time

    6.52   problem of life untouched by answering all possible scientific questions

    6.521   solution of problem of life lies in vanishing of problem

Like in Meaning (synonymous) [gleichbedeutend]

    4.243   if two words are like in meaning then to know them is to know that they have like meaning

Likeness [Gleichnis]

    4.012   sign such as aRb is a likeness of what is designated

    4.015   possibility of likenesses rests on logic of representation

    5.5563   simplest thing to give not likeness of truth but truth itself

Limit [Grenze]

    Foreword: Tractatus draws a limit to expression of thoughts; the limit is only in language

    5.143   contradiction is outer limit of propositions

    5.5561 empirical reality is limited by totality of objects

    5.6   limits of my language means limits of my world (See 5.62).

    5.61   limits of the world also limits of logic; to exclude certain possibilities logic must get outside limits of world

    5.62   world is my world in that limits of my language mean limits of my world

    5.632   subject is a limit of the world

    5.641   metaphysical subject (the philosophical I) a limit of the world

    6.43   willing may change limits of world

Limit [grenzen]

    4.112   philosophy should limit thoughts otherwise blurred

    4.113   philosophy limits disputable sphere of natural sciences

    4.114   philosophy limits thinkable and through it unthinkable

3.032   what contradicts logic cannot be presented in
          language

4.015   possibility of imagery rests on logic of imaging

4.0312   logic of derivative facts cannot stand as proxy for
          objects

4.1121   correspondence of study of sign-language to study of
          thought-processes in philosophy of logic

4.12   to be able to represent logical form, we should have
          to be able to put ourselves with propositions outside
          logic, outside world

4.126   confusion of formal and proper concepts runs through
          old logic

4.128   no pre-eminent numbers in logic

5.02   for Frege propositions of logic were names whose
          arguments were indices of these names

5.43   propositions of logic say same thing, nothing

5.45   if there are logical proto-signs, a correct logic must
          make clear their relative positions and justify their
          presence

5.451   if logic has fundamental concepts, these must be in-
          dependent of one another

5.452   introduction of new expedient in symbolism of logic
          must be consequential event

5.453   there are no numbers in logic

5.454   in logic there can be no classification

5.472   description of most general form of proposition is
          description of one general proto-sign of logic

5.473   what is possible in logic is also permitted; we cannot
          make mistakes in logic

5.4731   self-evidence can only be discarded in logic by
          language's preventing every logical mistake

5.511   logic can use special snags and manipulations though
          it is all-embracing mirror

5.551   every question logic can decide can be decided
          off-hand

5.552   experience needed to understand logic is not experi-
          ence that something is; logic precedes every experi-
          ence; logic is before the how, not the what

*   5.5521   question of logic and its application to world

Logic [Logik] continued   97

    6.127   all propositions of logic have equal rank

    6.1271   number of fundamental laws of logic is arbitrary

    6.13   logic not a doctrine but a mirror-image of world;
              logic is transcendental

    6.22   propositions of logic show in tautologies as mathe-
              matics shows in equations

    6.234   mathematics is a method of logic

    6.3   investigations of logic is investigation of conformity
              to law; outside logic all is accident

    6.342   relative position of logic and mechanics explained

Logic of Language [Sprachlogik]

    4.002   impossible to gather immediately logic of language
              from all colloquial language

    4.003   most propositions and questions on philosophical
              things senseless because logic of language not under-
              stood

Logical [logisch]

    1.13   derivative facts in logical space are the world

    2.0121   something logical cannot be merely possible

    2.0233   objects of same logical form are only differentiated
              by being different

    2.11   image presents state of affairs in logical space, the
              subsistence and non-subsistence of prime facts

    2.18   image, to image actuality at all, must have in common
              with it the logical form, that is, the form of actual-
              ity

    2.181   if form of imaging is logical form, image is called
              logical image

    2.182   every image is logical

    2.19   logical image can image world

    2.2   image shares logical form with imaged

    2.202   image represents possible state of affairs in logical
              space

    3.   logical image of derivative facts is the thought

    3.315   proposition whose signs are all changed into variables
              correspond to a logical form or proto-image

    3.325   sign-language needed which obeys rules of logical
              grammar and syntax

Logical [Logisch] continued

4.128   logical forms are anumerical

4.441   there are no logical objects

4.463   tautology leaves all logical space to actuality; contradiction fills it

4.465   logical product of tautology and proposition same as the proposition

4.466   logical union of their meanings corresponds to logical union of signs; to no logical union corresponds no union of objects

5.1362   connection of knowledge and known is that of logical necessity

5.152   certainty of logical conclusion is limiting case of probability

5.233   operation can first occur where proposition arises from another in logically meaningful way, where logical construction of propositions begins

5.2341   logical addition, logical multiplication, etc., are operations

5.4   logical objects, logical constants, in sense of Frege and Russell, do not exist

5.42   possibility of crosswise definition of logical proto-signs of Frege and Russell shows these are not proto-signs; designate no relationships

5.441   notation given for disappearnace of apparent logical constants

5.45   if there are logical proto-signs, a correct logic must make clear their relative positions and justify their presence

5.4541   solution of logical problems must be simple

* 5.46   sense of all combinations introduced with right logical signs

5.461   the apparently unimportant derivative fact that logical illusory relations like v need brackets is full of meaning

5.4611   logical operation signs are punctuations

5.47   all logical operations are contained in elementary propositions

5.4731   self-evidence can only be discarded in logic by language's preventing every logical mistake

5.47321   signs which serve one purpose are logically equivalent, which serve no purpose are logically meaningless

Logical [Logisch] continued

    6.2   mathematics is a logical method

    6.23   logical form of two expressions characterized by their being substitutable

    6.31   so-called law of induction not a logical law

    6.3211   a priori certainty is purely logical

    6.33   possibility of logical form is known a priori

    6.3431   physical laws still speak of objects of world through whole logical apparatus

    6.3631   process of induction has no logical, but only a psychological foundation

    6.37   there is only logical necessity

    6.374   there is no logical coherence between will and world to guarantee wishes

    6.375   as there is only logical necessity, so is there only logical impossibility

    6.3751   logical product of two elementary propositions can be neither tautology nor contradiction

Logical Symbolism. See Ideography

Logically [logisch]

    4.442   Frege's sign ⊢ is logically meaningless

    5.5563   propositions of colloquial language are logically in order taken just as they are

                   -M-

Make [machen]

    2.1   we make images of derivative facts for ourselves

    2.1513   imaging relation which makes image an image belongs to it

    3.001   we make image of prime fact, and this means that latter is thinkable

Man [Mensch]

    4.002   man possesses capacity for constructing languages in which every sense can be expressed

    5.641   philosophical I is not the man

    6.4312   temporal immortality of soul of man does not solve riddle of life in space and time, and is not assured

Mathematical [mathematisch] continued

6.233   language supplies necessary intuition for solution of mathematical problems

6.2341   essential of mathematical method is to work with equations

Mathematics [Mathematik]

5.43   scarcely to be believed that infinite number of propositions of logic (of mathematics) follow from half dozen "fundamental propositions"

6.031   theory of classes superfluous in mathematics; generality in mathematics not accidental

6.2   mathematics is a logical method; propositions of mathematics are equations, hence illusory propositions

6.21   propositions of mathematics express no thoughts

6.211   in life mathematics is needed only to infer from propositions that are not part of mathematics

6.22   mathematics shows logic of world in equations

6.2321   propositions of mathematics do not have to be compared with derivative facts as regards correctness

6.234   mathematics is a method of logic

6.2341   propositions of mathematics must be understood through themselves

6.24   mathematics arrives at its equations by method of substitution

Mauthner, Fritz

4.0031   his critique of language not the same as Wittgenstein's

Mean (refer to) [bedeuten]

3.203   name means the object

4.002   every sense capable of being expressed without knowing what each word means

4.111   word "philosophy" must mean something not standing beside natural science

4.115   philosophy will mean the unsayable by clearly representing the sayable

4.243   we cannot understand proposition in which two names occur without knowing whether they mean the same or different

4.3   truth-possibilities of elementary propositions mean possibility of existence of prime facts

5.6   limits of my language mean limits of my world (Cf. 5.62)

Merging [Zusammenfassung]

3.24   merging of symbols of complex into a simple symbol is expressible by a definition

Metaphysical [metaphysisch]

5.633   where in the world is a metaphysical subject?

5.641   philosophical I is the metaphysical subject, the limit of the world

6.53   right method of philosophy would be to say nothing except what can be said, and show that in metaphysical propositions certain signs lack meaning

Method [Methode]

3.11   method of projection is thinking of sense of proposition

4.1121   Wittgenstein's method has danger analogous to what entangled philosophers studying thought-processes

* 5.631   method of isolating subject, or showing it not to exist in book on world as I found it

* 6.1203   intuitive method for recognition of tautologies by using bracket notation

6.121   logical demonstration which combines propositions into propositions which say nothing is a zero-method

6.2   mathematics is a logical method. (Cf. 6.234.)

6.2341   essence of mathematical method is to work with equations; thus every proposition of mathematics must be understood through itself

6.24   mathematical method for arriving at equations is that of substitution

6.53   when someone wishes to say something metaphysical, demonstrate he has given no meaning to certain signs: this is right method of philosophy

Microcosm [Mikrokosmos]

5.63   I am my world, the microcosm

Minimum-Laws [Minimum-Gesetze]

6.321   in mechanics there are minimum-laws such as law of least action

Mirror [Spiegel]

5.511   special manipulations of logic connected to the great mirror by infinitely fine network

Mirror [spiegeln]

4.121   logical form mirrors itself in propositions; what mirrors itself in language, language cannot represent

Multiplicity [Mannigfaltigkeit] continued

    4.041   mathematical multiplicity cannot be imaged in turn

    4.0411   some expressions lack necessary multiplicity

    4.0412   idealist explanation of spatial relations fails to ex-
             plain their multiplicity

    5.475   system of signs with definite mathematical multipli-
             city needed to indicate number of fundamental opera-
             tions

Music [Musik]

    4.011   musical score does not at first appear to be image of
             music

Musical [musikalisch]

    3.141   musical theme is not a mixture of notes

    4.014   musical thought, score, waves of sound, all stand in
             imaging internal relation which holds between language
             and world

Mystical [das Mystische]

    6.44   not how world is but that it is, is the mystical

    6.45   feeling of world as limited whole is the mystical

    6.522   what cannot be enunciated shows itself, and is the
             mystical

                              -N-

Name [Name]

    3.142   a class of names cannot express a sense

    3.143   Frege called proposition a compound name

    3.144   names resemble points

    3.202   simple signs in propositions are called names

    3.203   the name means an object

    3.22   in proposition, name stands as proxy for an object

    3.26   name is a proto-sign; names cannot be dismembered by
             a definition (Cf. 3.261)

    3.3   name has meaning only in context of a proposition

    3.314   the variable name can be conceived as a propositional
             variable

Natural Science [Naturwissenschaft]. See also Mechanics; Science   111

    4.11   totality of true propositions is the total natural
            science

    4.111   philosophy is not a natural science; word "philosophy"
            means something above or below, but not beside,
            natural sciences

    4.1121   psychology no nearer philosophy than are the other
            natural sciences

    4.1122   Darwinian theory has no more to do with philosophy
            than has any other hypothesis of natural science

    4.113   philosophy limits disputable sphere of natural science

    6.4312   problems of natural science do not have to be solved
            in connection with immortality

    6.53   propositions of natural science are what can be said
            and have nothing to do with philosophy

Natural Science [naturwissenschaftlich]

    6.111   propositions of natural science and those of logic
            would be confused if "true" and "false" were taken as
            two properties, among others, of any proposition

Nature [Natur]

    2.023   collective possibilities of occurrence of objects in
            prime facts must be in nature of object

    3.315   class of propositions which are values of variable
            proposition depends on nature of the proposition

    5.47   logical constant is what all propositions, according
            to their nature, have in common

    6.124   in logic, nature of the necessary signs itself asserts

    6.34   propositions of continuity in nature, least expenditure
            in nature, etc., are insights into possible fashioning
            of propositions of science

Necessary [nötig]

    5.574   number of necessary fundamental operations depends
            only on notation

Necessary [notwendig]

    6.232   what is essential in equation is that it is not neces-
            sary to show that expressions it unites have same
            meaning

Necessity [Notwendigkeit]

    5.1362   connection of knowledge and known is that of logical
            necessity

New [neu]   113

    4.027   it lies in essence of proposition that it can communicate new sense

    4.03   proposition communicates new sense with old expressions

Newton, Sir Isaac. See also Hertz, Mechanics

    6.341   Newtonian mechanics brings description of world to unified form

  * 6.342   Newton's mechanics and description of world

No [nein]

    4.023   actuality fixed by proposition with respect to yes or no

Nonentity [Unding]

    5.5421   soul of contemporary psychology is a nonentity

Non-existence. See Non-subsistence

Non-proposition (pseudo-proposition) [Nichtsatz]

    5.5351   hypothesis for a non-proposition as argument is not false but nonsensical

Non-psychological [nicht-psychologisch]

    5.641   in philosophy we can talk of non-psychological I

Nonsense [Unsinn]

    Foreword: nonsense lies on other side of limit of language

    5.5303   to say two things are identical is nonsense

    5.5351   "p is a proposition" is nonsense; nonsense to place $p \supset p$ before a proposition to insure that its arguments have right form

    5.5422   correct explanation of "A judges p" must show it is impossible to judge a nonsense

    5.5571   if I cannot give elementary propositions a priori, to try to give them leads to nonsense

Nonsensical [unsinnig]. See also Senseless

    3.24   proposition which speaks of complex that does not exist is not nonsensical

    4.003   most propositions and questions about philosophic things are nonsensical

    4.124   a nonsensical to ascribe formal property to proposition as to deny it

Notation [Notation] continued

    3.3441   what is common to all notations for truth-functions
                can be expressed; a special possible notation can
                inform

    5.474   number of fundamental operations depends only on
                notation

    5.512   what is common to all signs for denial in notation
                is what denies

    5.513   even in Russell's notation "q: p v ~p" says "q"

    5.514   if notation is established, then rules for form-
                ing all propositions denying p, etc., are given

*   6.1203   notation given for form "~ξ"

    6.122   if notation is adequate, then properties of proposi-
                tions are known by mere inspection

    6.1223   logical truths can be postulated insofar as an ade-
                quate notation can be postulated

Novelty [Neuheit]

    Foreword: no claim made to novelty in details of Tractatus

Null. See Zero

Number [Anzahl]. See also entry following
    (Between Zahl and Anzahl - a collection - there is little to
    choose, in English, unfortunately, and our determination to
    translate them by separate words breaks down.)

    4.1272   nonsense to speak of number of all objects; expres-
                sions like "one is a number" are nonsense; number is
                a formal concept, represented by variable in ideog-
                raphy

    4.442   number of places in truth-conditions of proposition
                determined by number of members

    4.45   ordering of groups of truth-conditions belonging to
                truth-possibilities of a number of elementary proposi-
                tions

    5.101   truth-functions of every number of elementary proposi-
                tions given in schema

    5.32   all truth-functions are results of successive applica-
                tion of finite number of truth-operations to elemen-
                tary propositions

    5.43   it is scarcely to be believed that infinite number of
                propositions of logic (of mathematics) follow from
                half dozen "fundamental propositions"

Numerical Sign [Zahlenzeichen]

    4.126   numerical sign shows that it designates a number

-O-

Object [Gegenstand]. See also Entities; Things

    2.01   a prime fact is a union of objects

    2.0121   spatial objects unthinkable apart from space; any
                object unthinkable apart from union with other things;
                an object unthinkable apart from possibility of
                occurrence in prime fact

    2.0123   if object is known the possibility of occurrence in
                prime facts is known; every possibility lies in its
                nature

    2.01231   to know object its internal properties must be known

    2.0124   if all objects are given, all possible prime facts are
                given too

    2.0131   spatial object must lie in infinite space

    2.0131   object of touch must have a hardness

    2.014   objects contain possibility of all states of affairs

    2.0141   form of object is possibility of its occurrence in
                prime facts

    2.02   object is simple

    2.021   objects constitute the substance of the world

    2.023   fixed form consists of objects

    2.0231   configuration of objects presents material properties
                of the world

    2.0232   objects are colorless

    2.0233   two objects of same logical form differ from one
                another only by being different

    2.0251   space, time, and color are forms of objects

    2.026   only if there are objects can there be a fixed form of
                world

    2.027   object is one with the fixed and existent

    2.0271   object is the fixed, existent

Occurrence [Vorkommen] continued

> 5.25   occurrence of operation does not characterize sense
> of proposition

Old [alt]

> 4.03   proposition communicates new sense with old expression
>
> 4.126   confusion of formal and proper concepts runs through
> whole of old logic

Operation [Operation]

> 4.1273 general member of formal series determined by giving
> its first member and general form of generating opera-
> tion
>
> 5.21   internal relations of propositions may be represented
> by making a proposition a result of an operation pro-
> ducing it from other propositions
>
> 5.22   operation is expression of relation between its result
> and its bases
>
> 5.23   operation must happen to a proposition to make another
> proposition from it
>
> 5.232   internal relation ordering a series equivalent to
> operation
>
> 5.233   operation can first occur where logical construction
> of proposition begins
>
> 5.234   truth-functions of elementary propositions are results
> of truth-operations
>
> 5.2341 denial, logical addition, etc., are operations
>
> 5.24   operation shows itself in a variable
>
> 5.241   operation marks difference between forms
>
> 5.242   same operation makes q from p, r from q, etc.
>
> 5.25   operation does not assert, must not be mistaken for
> function
>
> 5.251   result of operation can be its own basis
>
> 5.2521 repeated application of operation to its own result
> called the successive application
>
> 5.2523 concept of successive application of operation equiva-
> lent to concept, etc.
>
> 5.253   operations cannot cancel each other
>
> 5.254   operations can disappear, as in double denial
>
> 5.4611 logical operation signs are punctuations

-P-

4.002   colloquial speech is part of human organism

5.634   no part of experience is a priori

5.641   philosophical I is not part of world

Particle [Teilchen]

6.3751   for particle to have two velocities at same time is a
logical impossibility

Passage [Ablauf]

6.3611   no process can be compared with passage of time
directly

Passage [Verlauf]

6.3611   description of temporal passage must be described from
standpoint of another procedure

Pattern [Gebilde]

4.0141   similarity between patterns seemingly different can
be found in a general rule, in music

5.4541   men have always felt there must be realm of questions
whose answers are united in close, regular pattern

Perceived [empfinden]

4.012   a proposition of the form aRb perceived as an image

Perceive [wahrnehmen]

5.5423   to perceive complex is to perceive relation of its
constituents

Perceptible [wahrnehmbar]

3.1   thought expresses itself in proposition perceptibly

3.11   sensibly perceptible sign of proposition is projection of possible state of affairs

3.32   sign is that which bears sense in what is perceptible
of the symbol

Phenomenon [Phänomen]

6.423   will as phenomenon interesting only to psychology

Philosophers [Philosophen]

Foreword: indifferent how far Wittgenstein's efforts agree
with those of other philosophers

4.003   most questions and propositions of philosophers result
from not understanding logic of language

124   Philosophers [Philosophen] continued

      4.1121   philosophers held study of thought processes essential to philosophy of logic

      4.122   philosophers often confuse internal and external relations

   Philosophic [philosophisch]

      Foreword: Tractatus treats philosophic problems

      4.003   most propositions and questions about philosophic things are nonsensical

      4.112   philosophic work consists essentially of elucidations; result of philosophy is not philosophic propositions but clarification of propositions

      4.128   there is no philosophic monism, etc.

      5.641   philosophic I is not man, soul, or body but a metaphysical subject

   Philosophy [Philosophie]

      3.324   philosophy full of confusions arising from misunderstanding of signs

      3.3421   in philosophy the possibility of every single thing is important

      4.0031   philosophy is critique of language

      4.111   philosophy not a natural science

      4.112   object of philosophy is clarification of thought; philosophy is not a doctrine but an activity; a work of philosophy consists of elucidations; philosophy should result in making propositions clear; philosophy should delimit and make clear thoughts otherwise turbid

      4.1121   psychology no closer to philosophy than are other natural sciences; theory of knowledge is philosophy of psychology; Wittgenstein's study of sign-language corresponds to study of thought-processes in philosophy of logic

      4.1122   Darwinian theory no more relevant to philosophy than is any other hypothesis of natural sciences

      4.113   philosophy limits disputable sphere of natural science

      4.114   philosophy should limit unthinkable through thinkable

      4.115   philosophy will mean unspeakable by clearly representing the speakable

      5.641   I enters philosophy as a metaphysical subject

      6.113   whole philosophy of logic contained in self-evidence of logical propositions

Philosophy [Philosophie] continued

    6.211   question of why we use word or proposition leads to
                insights in philosophy

* 6.53   the right method of philosophy described

Phonetic Spelling [Lautzeichenschrift]

    4.011   at first phonetic spelling does not seem image of
                spoken language

Phonograph Record [Grammophonplatte]

    4.014   internal imaging relation between phonograph record
                and score, musical thought and sound waves, like that
                between language and world

    4.0141   rule by which to reconstruct symphony from groove on
                phonograph record; rule of translation projects score-
                language into that of phonograph record

Physical [physikalisch]

    6.3431   physical laws through their logical apparatus speak
                of objects of world

    6.374   physical connection between world and will could not
                be willed

Physics [Physik]

    3.0321   laws of physics could be contradicted by prime fact

    6.321   in physics there are causal laws

    6.341   system of mechanics must enable one to write any
                proposition of physics

    6.3751   logical impossibility formulated in terms of physics

Picture. See Image

Picturing. See Imagery, Imaging

Place [Stelle]. See also Locus; Space

    4.442   number of places expressing number of truth-conditions
                of propositions determined by number of members in
                proposition

    5.452   place of new device in logical symbolism must be
                clarified

    6.112   logical propositions hold unique place among all
                propositions

* 6.342   relative place of logic and mechanics explained

Position [Lage] continued   127

6.35   geometry can say nothing about factual position of
          spots in image

Positive [positiv]

2.06   existence of prime fact called a positive derivative
          fact

4.063   black spots on paper correspond to positive derivative
          facts

4.463   proposition, image, model, are in positive sense like
          space limited by solid substance in which body has a
          place

5.5151   negative proposition must presuppose positive proposi-
          tion, and conversely

Possibility [Möglichkeit]

2.012   possibility that a thing can occur in a prime fact

2.0121   no object can be thought of apart from possibility of
          union with others

2.0123   if object is known, all possibilities of occurrence
          in prime fact also known; every possibility must lie
          in nature of object

2.014   objects contain possibility of all states of affairs

2.0141   form of object is its possibility of occurrence in
          prime fact

2.033   form is possibility of structure

2.15   possibility of structure of image is form of imaging

2.151   that things related as elements of image are in the
          form of imaging

2.201   possibility of existence and non-existence of prime
          fact is what the image images

2.203   image contains possibility of state of affairs

3.02   thought contains possibility of state of affairs

3.04   an a priori correct thought would be one whose pos-
          sibility conditioned its truth

3.13   possibility of what is projected belongs to proposi-
          tion; possibility of expressing its sense is contained
          in proposition, but not sense itself

3.23   postulate of possibility of simple signs relates to
          definiteness of sense

3.3421   possibility of every single thing reveals something
          about essense of world

Possible [möglich] continued

130   Possible [möglich]

      6.125   possible to give description of all "true" logical
                propositions at outset

      6.34   laws are a priori insight into possible fashioning
                of propositions of science

      6.3611   description of temporal sequences is possible

      6.52   if all possible scientific questions are answered,
                problem of life remains untouched, though no questions
                are left

Postulate [fordern]

      6.1223   logical truths can be postulated insofar as we postu-
                late adequate notation

Postulate [Forderung]

      3.23   postulate of possibility of simple single signs is
                postulate of determinateness of sense

Practical [praktisch]

      5.47321 Occam's Razor is not justified by its practical success

Predicate [Prädikat]

      4.1274   one cannot ask if there are unanalyzable subject-
                predicate propositions

Pre-eminent [ausgezeichnet]

      4.128   no pre-eminent numbers in logic

      5.453   there are no pre-eminent numbers

Prejudged [präjudiziert]

      2.012   possibility of prime fact in which a thing can occur
                is prejudged in that thing

      5.44   possibility of denial is prejudged in affirmation

Preliminary [Vorbereitung]

      4.0641   that one can deny denied proposition shows that what
                is denied is proposition, not its preliminary

Present [Gegenwart]

      6.4311   if eternity is timelessness, then he lives eternally
                who lives in the present

Present [gegenwärtig]

      6.4312   is not eternal life as enigmatic as our present one?

Presenting [vorstellend]

      5.631   there is no thinking, presenting subject

Prime Fact (atomic fact, relation of entities, elementary state)
[Sachverhalt]
(Here again the German has no obvious equivalent; but even
apart from this, Wittgenstein's concept seems to admit of
several different interpretations. As with "Derivative
Fact," our rendering is rather arbitrary, and certainly no
more than an· approximation.)

2.   subsistence of prime facts is the derivative facts

2.01   prime fact is union of objects

2.011   essential to thing that it can be a constituent of
            prime fact

2.012   possibility of prime fact prejudged in thing which
            can occur in it

2.0121   if things can occur in prime facts, this possibility
            must already be in the things; if I can think of
            object in union of prime fact, I cannot think of it
            apart from possibility of this

2.0122   form of independence of thing is form of coherence
            in prime fact

2.0123   if object is known its possible occurence in prime
            facts is known

2.0124   all possible prime facts are given if objects are
            given

2.013   everything is in a space of possible prime facts

2.0141   form of object is possibility of occurrence in prime
            facts

2.0272   configuration of objects forms prime fact

2.03   objects hang together in prime fact

2.031   objects are related in definite way in prime fact

2.032   structure of prime fact is way objects cohere in it

2.034   structure of derivative fact consists of structures
            of prime facts

2.04   totality of subsistent prime facts is world

2.05   totality of subsistent prime facts determines which
            ones do not subsist

2.06   the subsistence and non-subsistence of prime facts is
            actuality; their subsistence is a positive fact, their
            non-subsistence a negative one

2.061   prime facts are independent of one another

2.062   subsistence or non-subsistence of one prime fact tells
            nothing about others

Probable [wahrscheinlich]

    5.153   proposition is in itself neither probable nor improbable

* 5.154   what it means to say that two events are equally probable explained

Probability [Wahrscheinlichkeit]

* 5.15   measure of probability formulated for shared truth-grounds of two propositions

* 5.151   probability which one proposition gives to another explained in formula

    5.152   independent propositions give to each other the probability one-half; certainty of logical conclusion is limiting case of probability

* 5.154   image of urn and white and black balls used to explain probability of independent events

    5.155   degree of probability given to occurrence of event by circumstances is unit of probability proposition

    5.156   probability is a generalization

Probability Proposition [Wahrscheinlichkeitssatz]

    5.1511 no special object proper to probability propositions

    5.155   unit of probability proposition is degree of probability given to occurrence of event by circumstances

    5.156   probability proposition is extract from other propositions

Probability Theory [Wahrscheinlichkeitslehre]

    4.464   indication of gradations needed for probability theory

    5.1   that truth-functions can be ordered in series is foundation of probability theory

Problem [Problem]

    Foreword: Tractatus treats philosophic problems, showing that they rest on misapprehension of logic of language; problems in essentials solved, but little has been done when they are solved

    4.003   the deepest problems are really no problems

    5.4541 solutions of logical problems must be simple for they set standard of simplicity

    5.535   problems connected with illusory propositions disappear in correct logical notation

Projection [Projektion]   135

    3.11   sign of proposition used as projection of possible
               state of affairs; method of projection is thinking
               of sense of proposition

    3.13   everything belonging to projection belongs to proposi-
               tion; possibility of what is projected belongs to
               proposition

    4.0141   law of projection is general rule which projects
               symphony into language of score

Projective [projektiv]

    3.12   proposition is propositional sign in projective rela-
               tion to world

Proof [Beweis]

    6.126   proof of logical propositions is creating them from
               others by certain operations

    6.1262   proof in logic a mechanical expedient

    6.1263   logical proof of sense-bearing proposition and proof
               in logic are different

    6.1264   proof of sense-bearing proposition shows that it is
               so; in logic every proposition is the form of a proof

    6.1265   every proposition in logic is its own proof

 * 6.241   proof of the proposition "2 x 2 = 4" in notational
               form

Proper (real) [eigentlich]

    3.3411   proper name is that which all symbols signifying
               object have in common

    4.122   confusion between internal and proper relations

    4.1272   variable name "x" is proper sign of illusory concept
               "object"; where "object" is used as proper concept-
               word, nonsense results

Proper Concept [eigentlicher Begriff]. See also Concept; Formal
   Concept

    4.126   proper concept confused with formal concept; in old
               logic proper concept can be presented by a function

Properly [eigentlich]

    4.003   deepest problems are properly no problems

Property [Eigenschaft]. See also Formal Property

    2.01231 internal and external properties of object must be
               known

Property [Eigenschaft] continued   137

6.121   logical properties of propositions demonstrated by
         propositions of logic

6.122   in adequate notation formal properties of propositions
         are known by mere inspection

6.126   whether proposition belongs to logic can be calculated
         through logical properties of symbol

6.231   a property of affirmation is that it can be conceived
         as double denial

6.35   properties of geometrical network can be given a priori

Proposition (sentence, statement) [Satz]. <u>See also</u> Assertion;
    Elementary Proposition; Fundamental <u>Proposition</u>; General Propo-
    sition; Propositional Sign
    (Most positivists would no doubt translate Satz as "sentence";
    we believe, however, in view of the fact that for Wittgen-
    stein the Satz is partly hidden from view and not wholly an
    overt sign, that it conforms better to a rather common usage
    of the word "proposition." But even so, the word Satz has
    more than one meaning in the <u>Tractatus</u>.)

2.0122   words cannot occur both alone and in proposition

2.0201   analysis of statement about complex yields proposi-
         tions describing complexes

2.0211   if there were no substance, sense of proposition would
         depend on truth of another proposition

2.0231   material properties are first presented by proposi-
         tions

3.1   proposition expresses thought perceptibly through
         senses

3.11   sign of proposition a projection of possible state of
         affairs; method of projection is thinking the sense
         of proposition

3.12   proposition is propositional sign in its projective
         relation to world

3.13   to proposition belongs all that belongs to projection;
         sense not contained in proposition, only possibility
         of expressing it; content of proposition means content
         of sense-bearing propositions; form of sense of propo-
         sition is contained, but not content

3.141   proposition not a mixture of words; it is articulated

3.143   in printed proposition, sign of proposition not essen-
         tially different from word; hence Frege called propo-
         sition a compounded name

Proposition [Satz] continued

3.323   in colloquial language two words signifying differently are often apparently applied in the same way in propositions

3.332   no proposition can say anything about itself, because propositional sign cannot contain itself

3.333   if function could be its own argument, outer and inner function must have different meanings

3.34   proposition possesses essential and accidental features

3.341   what is common to all propositions which can express same sense is essential to the proposition

3.4   proposition determines a locus in logical space, which is guaranteed by significant proposition

3.42   proposition determines only one place in logical space, but whole logical space is given with it; proposition reaches through the whole logical space

4.   the thought is the sense-bearing proposition

4.001   totality of propositions is the language

4.003   most propositions about philosophic things not false, but nonsensical

4.0031 apparent logical form of proposition need not be actual one

4.01   proposition is an image of actuality; it is a model of actuality as we think it is

4.011   at first, proposition does not seem to be image of actuality

4.012   proposition of the form aRb perceived as image

4.016   to understand essence of proposition one should consider hieroglyphics

4.021   proposition an image of actuality; understood if I know state of affairs presented by it; understood without having its sense explained

4.022   proposition shows its sense; proposition shows how things relate, if it is true; if true, shows how things stand; says that they stand so

4.023   actuality must be fixed by proposition with respect to yes or no; proposition is the description of a prime fact; describes actuality through its internal properties; constructs world with help of logical scaffolding; conclusions from false proposition possible

4.11	totality of true propositions is total natural science
4.112	result of philosophy is not philosophical propositions, but clarification of propositions
4.12	proposition can represent total actuality, but not what they have in common with it, the logical form; to represent logical form, proposition would be outside logic and world
4.121	logical form mirrors and exhibits itself in proposition
4.1211	contradictions of propositions shown in structure; and inferential relation shown also
4.122	proposition cannot assert subsistence of internal properties and relations, but these show themselves within propositions
4.124	nonsensical to ascribe or deny formal property to a proposition
4.126	that anything falls under a formal concept cannot be expressed by proposition
4.1272	use of word "object" etc., as proper concept leads to illusory propositions
4.1273	generation of successive propositions by use of general term of formal series
4.1274	no proposition can answer question of existence of formal concept
4.2	sense of proposition is its agreement and disagreement with possibilities of subsistence or non-subsistence of prime fact
4.21	simplest proposition, the elementary proposition, asserts subsistence of a prime fact
* 4.243	whether we understand proposition having two names without knowing if the names have same or different meaning
4.4	proposition is an expression of agreement and disagreement with truth-possibilities of elementary propositions
4.411	understanding of propositions requires introduction of elementary propositions; of general propositions depends on that of elementary propositions
4.42	possibilities formulated for agreement and disagreement of propositions with truth-possibilities of n elementary propositions

5.124   proposition affirms every proposition which follows
           from it

5.1241   two propositions are opposed if there is no sense-
           bearing proposition which both assert; every propo-
           sition which contradicts another denies it

5.13   truth of one proposition following from truth of
           others is perceived from structure of propositions

5.131   if truth of one proposition follows from truth of
           others, relations of these propositions are internal

5.1311   relation between forms of propositions can be con-
           cealed by method of designating

5.132   inference from one proposition to another is to be
           grasped from the propositions alone

5.1363   if it does not follow from a proposition's being
           evident that it is true, then evidence is no justi-
           fication for belief in its truth

5.14   if one proposition follows from another, then it says
           less than the other

5.141   if p follows from q and q from p, they are same propo-
           sition

5.142   tautology follows from all propositions

5.143   contradiction is outer limit of proposition, tautology
           its substanceless center

5.15   probability formula given for proposition which shares
           truth-grounds with another

5.151   probability which one proposition gives to another
           explained in formula

5.152   propositions which have no truth-arguments in common
           are mutually independent; if p follows from q, then
           proposition q gives p the probability one

5.153   proposition is in itself neither probable nor im-
           probable

5.156   proposition is always a complete image, but can be
           incomplete image of a certain state of affairs

5.2   structures of propositions stand in internal relations

5.21   internal relations of structures of propositions can
           be displayed by representing propositions as results
           of operation which produces it from other propositions

5.23   operation is what must happen to proposition to make
           another out of it

* 5.512   assertion and denial of propositions and their agree-
           ment with reality

  5.513   propositions opposed when they have nothing in common;
           every proposition has only one negative

  5.514   if notation is fixed, then it has a rule for construct-
           ing all propositions which, e.g., negate or affirm p

  5.515   proposition is what is connected by logical constants

  5.5151   negative and positive propositions interrelated

  5.521   it is difficult to understand propositions in which
           ideas of logical product and logical sum lie concealed
           according to Frege's and Russell's introduction of
           generality

  5.525   possibility or impossibility of a state of affairs is
           expressed by whether propositions are sense-bearing or
           not

  5.526   one can describe world completely by completely gen-
           eralized propositions

  5.5261   a completely generalized proposition is composite

  5.5262   truth or falsehood of every proposition alters some-
           thing in structure of world; totality of elementary
           ones is what the completely general ones delimit

  5.5302   a proposition saying that two objects have all proper-
           ties in common has sense

  5.5351   nonsense to place p ⊃ p before proposition to ensure
           that arguments have right form

  5.54   proposition occurs in the general propositional form
           only as basis of truth-operations

  5.541   propositions like "A says 'p'" are not truth-functions
           of p, though so conceived in modern epistemology

  5.5422   correct clarification of form of proposition "A judges
           p" must show it is impossible to judge nonsense

  5.551   fundamental proposition is that anything decidable by
           logic requires nothing further

  5.5562   knowing proposition in unanalyzed form implied by
           knowledge of elementary propositions on logical
           grounds

  5.5563   propositions of colloquial language are already in
           order logically

* 6.   general form of proposition formulated in notation

  6.001   every proposition the result of successive application
           of operation N'($\bar{\xi}$) to elementary propositions

Proposition [Satz] continued   147

6.1265   logic can be so conceived that every proposition is
         its own proof

6.127   propositions of logic are equal in rank

6.1271   Frege should not have appealed to self-evidence as
         criterion of logical proposition

6.2   propositions of mathematics are equations, hence
         illusory propositions

6.21   propositions of mathematics express no thoughts

6.211   mathematical propositions never needed in life, but
         are used for inference; "Why do we use that word,
         that proposition?" is question in philosophy leading
         to valuable insights

6.22   propositions of logic show in tautologies what propo-
         sitions of mathematics show in equations about logic
         of world

6.2321   correctness of propositions of mathematics can be seen
         without comparing them to derivative facts

6.2341   propositions of mathematics must be understood through
         themselves

6.31   so-called law of induction is a sense-bearing proposi-
         tion

6.34   propositions such as principle of reason are a priori
         insights into world

6.341   mechanics determines form of world description by de-
         manding that all propositions used in world descrip-
         tion come from a number of given propositions; one
         must be able to write any proposition of physics in
         mechanics

6.343   mechanics attempts to construct all true propositions
         according to a single plan

6.4   all propositions are of equal value

6.42   there can be no propositions of ethics; propositions
         can express nothing higher

6.53   method of philosophy should be to demonstrate that
         certain signs in metaphysical propositions have no
         meaning

6.54   Wittgenstein's propositions elucidate because to
         understand them is finally to recognize them as non-
         sensical

Propositional Union [Satzverband]   149

4.221   question arises, how propositional union comes to be

Propositional Variable [Satzvariable]. See also Variable

3.313   when a variable becomes a constant, and the expression
         is a proposition, the variable is a propositional
         variable

3.314   every variable can be conceived as propositional
         variable

3.316   values of propositional variable fixed

3.317   fixing values of propositional variable is declaration
         of propositions whose common mark the variable is; de-
         termination of values of propositional variable is
         description of these propositions

4.126   expression of formal concept is a propositional varia-
         ble

4.127   values of propositional variable designate objects
         falling under concept

5.502   notation for negation of all values of propositional
         variable

Proto-image (primitive sign, archetype, prototype) [Urbild]. See
   also Proto-sign

3.24   notion of generality contains proto-image

3.315   class of propositions which are values of variable
         proposition corresponds to logical proto-image

3.333   functional sign contains logical proto-image of its
         own argument

5.522   sign of generality refers to logical proto-image

5.5351   temptation to use expressions like "a = a" in speaking
         of proto-images

Proto-sign (primitive sign) [Urzeichen]. See also Proto-image

3.26   name cannot be dismembered by a definition, as it is
         a proto-sign

3.261   a proto-sign and a sign defined by proto-signs cannot
         designate in the same way

3.263   meanings of proto-signs can be clarified by elucida-
         tions, which are propositions containing the proto-
         signs, and can be understood only when the meanings
         of these signs are already known

5.42   possibility of crosswise definition of the logical
         proto-signs of Frege and Russell shows that these are
         not proto-signs

Purpose [Zweck]

  3.341   essential in a symbol is what symbols must have in
           order to fulfill same purpose

  4.002   external form of language constructed with purpose
           other than to let form of thought be recognized

  5.47321 signs which serve one purpose are logically equiva-
           lent; signs which serve no purpose are logically
           meaningless

  5.5351   proposition survives wrong arguments no better and no
           worse than senseless hypothesis attached to it for
           this purpose

  6.1202   contradictions as well as tautologies could be used
           to show properties of structure of propositions

Put Together [zusammengestellt]

  4.031   in proposition state of affairs is put together tenta-
           tively

                                -Q-

Question [Frage]. See also Problem; Riddle

  4.003   most questions about philosophical things are not
           false but nonsense; these questions cannot be an-
           swered; they result from not understanding logic of
           language; questions are like whether good is more
           identical than the beautiful

  5.1251   question whether all relationships are internal or
           external vanishes

  4.1274   question about existence of formal concept is non-
           sense; no proposition can answer it

  5.45411 men have always felt there must be realm of questions
           whose answers a priori are symmetrical

  5.55   question about all possible forms of elementary propo-
           sitions

  5.551   every question that logic can decide can be decided
           offhand

  5.5542   "What must be in order that anything can be the
           case" - has this question any sense?

  5.62   key provided to question of truth of solipsism

  6.1222   light thrown on question of why logical propositions
           can no more be confirmed than refuted by experience

Realm [Gebiet] continued

    5.4541   men have always felt there must be realm of questions
               whose answers a priori are symmetrical, realm in which
               proposition, simplex sigillum veri, holds

Reckoning. See Calculating

Recognize [erkennen]

    2.223   truth of picture recognized through comparison with
              actuality

    2.224   truth or falsehood not recognized through image alone

    3.05   we would recognize a priori true thought through
              throught alone

    4.002   form of body not recognized through form of clothes

Recognition [das Erkennen]

    6.1262   proof in logic an expedient for recognition of tau-
               tology

Refer. See Mean

Reference. See Meaning

Regularity. See Conformity to Law

Related (combined) [verhalten]

    2.031   in the prime fact objects are related in a definite
              manner

    2.14   elements in image are related in a definite manner

    2.15   that elements in image are related, represents that
              things are so related

    2.151   form of imaging is possibility that things are related
              as are elements in image

    3.14   elements of propositional sign are related in definite
              manner, and this is the propositional sign

    5.5423   perceiving a complex in perceiving that its constitu-
              ents are related in a definite manner

Relation [Beziehung]. See also Relationship

    2.1513   imaging relation also belongs to image

    2.1514   imaging relation consists of co-ordinations of
              elements in image and entities

    3.12   proposition is propositional sign in projective rela-
              tion to world

Relationship [Relation] continued   155

    4.125   existence of internal relationship between possible
                states of affairs expressed by an internal relation-
                ship between propositions

    4.1251   question "whether all relationships are internal or
                external" vanishes

    4.1252   series ordered by internal relationships called formal
                series; number-series ordered by internal relation-
                ships

    5.232   internal relationship which orders series is equiva-
                lent to operation

    5.242   p, q, r, etc., are variables which give general expres-
                sion to certain formal relationships

    5.42   possibility of crosswise definition of logical "proto-
                signs" of Frege and Russell shows that these designate
                no relationships

    5.5301   identity is not a relationship between objects

    5.541   in "A says p" it appears superficially as if proposi-
                tion stood in relationship to object

    5.553   simple relationships between different numbers of
                things claimed by Russell

    5.5541   possible need for sign of a 27-term relationship
                should be decidable a priori

Replaced [ersetzt]

    3.344   what designates in symbol is what is common to all
                symbols replaced according to rules of logical syntax

Represent (present) [darstellen]

    2.0231   material properties first represented by propositions

    2.173   image represents its object from without, hence
                rightly or falsely

    2.201   the image images by representing possibility of exist-
                ence of prime facts

    2.202   image represents a possible state of affairs in logi-
                cal space

    2.203   image contains possibility of state of affairs which
                it represents

    2.22   the image images what it represents through form of
                imaging

    2.221   image represents its sense

Represent (present) [darstellen] continued   157

   5.21   internal relations of structures of propositions can
             be displayed if we represent proposition as result of
             operation which produces it from other propositions

* 6.1203   sign which represents p ⊃ q given in bracket-notation

   6.124   logical propositions represent scaffolding of world

   6.1264   every proposition of logic is a <u>modus</u> <u>ponens</u> repre-
             sented in signs

   6.3751   contradiction of two colors in one place represents
             itself in physics through impossibility for particle
             to have two velocities at one time

Representation [Darstellung]

   2.174   image cannot place itself outside its form of repre-
             sentation

   4.242   expressions of form "a = b" are only expedients in
             representation

Resolution [Auflösung]

   3.3442   resolution of sign of complex would be different in
             every propositional structure

Result [Resultat]

   4.112   result of philosophy is not propositions but their
             clarification

   5.21   internal relations of structures of propositions can
             be displayed by representing proposition as result of
             operation which produces it from other propositions

   5.22   operation is expression of relation between structures
             of its results and its bases

   5.234   truth-functions of elementary propositions are results
             of operations having elementary propositions as bases

   5.25   only result of operation asserts, and this depends on
             bases

   5.251   result of operation can be its own basis

   5.2521   repeated application of operation to its result called
             "successive application"

   5.3   every proposition is result of truth-operations on
             elementary propositions

   5.32   all truth-functions are results of successive applica-
             tion of finite number of truth-operations to elemen-
             tary propositions

Rule [Regel] continued   159

Russell, Bertrand

160   Russell, Bertrand continued

    5.521   introduced generality in connection with logical
             product

    5.525   his rendering of (℈x).fx not correct

    5.5302   wrongness of his definition of " = " explained

    5.535   place to solve problems arising from his axiom of
             infinity found

    5.5351   he renders the nonsense "p is a proposition" in sym-
             bols in Principles of Mathematics

    5.541   his conception of propositions like "A says p" men-
             tioned

    5.5422   his theory does not satisfy condition for explanation
             of propositions like "A says p"

    5.553   he said there were simple relations between different
             numbers of things

    6.123   his supposal of special law of contradiction for every
             logical type is wrong

    6.1232   his Axiom of Reducibility not a logical proposition

                              -S-

Said [gesagt]. See also Say

    Foreword: what can be said can be said clearly

    4.1212   what can be shown cannot be said

    6.51   questions and answers exist only where something can
             be said

Sameness [Gleichheit]. See also Equilibrium; Equal in Value;
    Equation; Identity; Like; Likeness; Sign of Equality

    5.53   sameness of object expressed by sameness of sign

    5.5301   sign of sameness needed to express relation of a to a

Say [sagen]. See also Enunciate; Express; Speak; Talk

    3.031   we could not say of "unlogical" world how it would
             look

    3.221   proposition can only say how a thing is, not what

    4.022   proposition says things as it shows them to be, if it
             is true

Say [sagen] continued

Sayable [Sagbar]

Scaffolding [Gerüst]

Scale. See Measuring Stick

Scepticism [Skeptizismus]

Schema [Schema]

Science [Wissenschaft]. See also Mechanics; Natural Science

162 Scientific [wissenschaftlich]

> 6.341   the scientific edifice is constructed from bricks supplied by mechanics
>
> 6.52   when all possible scientific questions are answered, problem of life is still untouched

Scope [Bereich]

> 4.0411 scope of generalization cannot be fixed internally

Score [Notenschrift]

> 4.011   at first score does not appear to be image of music
>
> 4.013   use of sharps and flats an example of apparent irregularities in score
>
> 4.014   score stands to phonograph record, musical thought, waves of sound, in same relation as that holding between language and world

See [sehen]

> 6.342   now we see the relative position of logic and mechanics
>
> 6.54   one must surmount the propositions of the Tractatus to see the world correctly

Self-Dependent [selbständig]

> 2.0122 thing is self-dependent

Self-Evidence [Einleuchten]

> 5.4731 self-evidence can be done away with in logic if language prevents each logical mistake
>
> 6.1271 Frege's criterion of self-evidence in logical propositions mistaken

Sense [Sinn]. See also Meaning; Nonsense; Senseless
(There can be no doubt of the translation of this term, which in both its German and English dress permits Wittgenstein, by a kind of punning, to attribute "sense," "significance," to a proposition, and to liken the proposition to an arrow pointing, like a vector, toward a recognizable state of affairs.)

> * Foreword: sense of Tractatus summed up in two statements
>
> 2.0211 in a world without substance sense of proposition would depend on truth of another proposition
>
> 2.221   image represents its sense
>
> 2.222   truth of image consists in agreement of sense with actuality

Sense [Sinn] continued 163

3.11 method of projecting possible is thinking sense of propositions

3.13 in proposition sense is not contained but possibility of expressing sense; proposition contains form of sense

3.142 only a derivative fact, not a class of names, can express a sense

3.1431 sense of proposition represented through mutual spatial location of objects

3.144 propositions resemble arrows in having sense

3.23 postulate of definiteness of sense is postulate of possibility of simple signs

3.3 only proposition has sense

3.31 every part of a proposition which characterizes sense called an expression; expression is everything essential for sense of proposition which propositions can have in common

* 3.328 sense of Occam's Razor explained

3.34 essential features of propositions are those enabling it to express sense

3.341 essential in proposition is common to all propositions expressing same sense

4.002 every sense can be expressed in language

4.011 sign languages prove to be images in ordinary sense of word

4.02 sense of propositional sign understood without being explained

4.021 proposition is understood without having its sense explained

4.022 proposition shows its sense

4.027 in essence of the proposition that it can communicate new sense

4.03 proposition communicates new sense with old words

4.031 instead of saying proposition has sense one could say it represents state of affairs

4.032 sense changes if proposition "ambulo" receives another stem or ending

Sense [Sinn] continued

    5.5302   proposition that two objects have all properties in
                 common has sense

*   5.5542   whether question of what must be for something to be
                 the case has sense

    6.124   logical propositions presuppose that elementary propo-
                 sitions have sense

    6.126   logical propositions formed without trouble about sense

*   6.232   Frege's distinction between meaning and sense

    6.41   sense of world must be outside world

    6.422   ethics has nothing to do with punishment and reward in
                 ordinary sense

    6.521   reason that one cannot say in what the sense of life
                 consists

Sense-bearing (significant) [sinnvoll]
    (English lacks an adjective to indicate that something has sense
    of the kind Wittgenstein intends. "Sensitive," "sensive," "sen-
    sible," "sensate," lead off in other directions. Our translation
    is awkward, but so is any neologism like "sensical." "Signifi-
    cant" does not make clear the textual connections of the word.)

    3.313   "content of proposition" means content of sense-bearing
                 proposition

    3.4   existence of logical locus of proposition assured by
                 existence of constituents, the existence of sense-bear-
                 ing propositions

    3.326   to recognize symbol in sign consider the sense-bearing
                 use

    4.   the thought is the sense-bearing proposition

    5.1241   two propositions are opposed if there is no sense-
                 bearing proposition which both assert

    5.525   possibility of some state of affairs is expressed by
                 this, that an expression is a sense-bearing proposition

    6.1263   logical proof of sense-bearing proposition and proof
                 in logic differ

    6.1264   proof of a sense-bearing proposition shows that it is
                 one

    6.31   so-called law of induction is a sense-bearing propo-
                 sition

Setting Up [Aufstellung]

   * 6.422   one's first thought in setting up an ethical law

Show [zeigen]

      Foreword: Tractatus shows how philosophic problems rest upon misapprehension of logic of language; it shows how little has been done when problems have been solved

      2.02331 impossible to show any one object if it has all its properties in common with others

      4.0031 Russell has shown that apparent logical form need not be actual form

      4.022 proposition shows its sense; proposition if true shows how things are related

      4.0621 that p and ~p can say same thing show that "~" corresponds to nothing

      4.063 black spot on white paper can be shown without knowing what white and black are, but truth of proposition cannot be shown without determining when it is true

      4.0641 denying a denied proposition shows that what is denied is already a proposition

      4.121 proposition shows logical form of actuality

      4.1211 proposition fa shows that object a occurs in its sense

      4.1212 what can be shown cannot be said

      4.122 expressions introduced to show ground of confusion between internal and external relations; existence of internal properties and relations shows for itself

      4.126 name shows that it signifies an object

      4.243 that expressions like a = a are not sense-bearing signs will show itself later

      4.442 Frege's assertion sign only shows he holds propositions so marked are true

      4.461 proposition shows what it says, tautologies and contradictions show that they say nothing

      5.1311 fact of inference can show generality in symbol

      5.24 operation shows itself in variable

      5.515 our symbols must show that v, etc., connect propositions

      5.5261 that generalized proposition is composite is shown by notation

Sign (symbol) [Zeichen] continued

5.473   a possible sign must be able to designate

5.4732   sign cannot be given wrong sense

5.47321   signs with one purpose are logically equivalent, signs with no purpose meaningless

5.475   system of signs having definite multiplicity gives number of fundamental operations

5.501   sign of form "(ξ)" indicates expression in brackets whose members are propositions

5.512   what negates in ~p is what all signs in notation which negate p have in common

5.515   sign p in p v q to have sense must stand for a complex sign

5.5151   sign of negative proposition constructed from sign of positive proposition

5.53   identity or difference of signs expresses identity or difference of objects

5.5301   sign of sameness needed to express that "a" has relation to "a" which satisfies function f

5.533   sign of identity is not a constituent logical notation

5.5541   possible need for sign of 27-term relation would be decidable a priori

5.5542   impossible to set out sign form and not know whether anything can correspond to it

* 6.02   rule of signs for defining numbers in terms of series

* 6.1203   sign of p ⊃ q in terms of T, F, and transverse brackets

6.124   in logic, nature of the essentially necessary signs asserts itself

6.1264   a proposition of logic is a modus ponens represented in signs

6.53   right method of philosophy would be to say nothing except what can be said; and when someone wished to say something metaphysical, to demonstrate that he had given no meaning to certain signs in his propositions

           Notation; Symbolism
           (The alternative translations are incorrect, contravening as
           they do Wittgenstein's distinct usages.)

           3.325   sign language must obey logical syntax by not applying
                    same sign in different symbols

           3.343   every correct sign language is translatable

           4.11   sign languages prove to be images even in ordinary
                    sense

           4.1121   Wittgenstein's study of sign language faces danger
                    analogous to that in study of thought-processes

           4.5   general form of proposition a description of propo-
                    sitions of one sign language

           6.124   propositions of logic given with logical syntax of
                    sign language

      Sign of Addition. See Addition Sign

      Sign of Assertion. See Assertion Sign

      Sign of Equality [Gleichheitzeichen]

           3.323   word "is" can be used as sign of equality

           6.23   two expressions connected by sign of equality are
                    substitutable

        * 6.232   what is essential in equation containing sign of
                    equality

      Sign of Generality. See Designation of Generality

      Sign Rule [Zeichenregel]

        * 6.02   sign rules given for writing numbers

           6.126   logical propositions formed out of others by sign
                    rules

      Sign-union [Zeichenverbinding]

           5.451   unless fundamental concept is introduced for all
                    cases, there is no reason to use same method of
                    sign-union in two cases

      Significant. See Sense-bearing

      Signify. See Designate

      (be) Silent [schweigen]

           7.   on that of which one cannot speak, one must be silent

Similarity [Ähnlichkeit]

> 4.0141   similarity of symphony and score is a law of projection
>
> 5.231   operation will depend on internal similarity of forms of propositions

Simple [einfach]

> 2.02   object is simple
>
> 3.201   elements of propositional sign which correspond to objects are called "simple signs"
>
> 3.202   simple signs in propositions are called names
>
> 3.21   to configuration of simple signs corresponds configuration of objects
>
> 3.23   postulate of possibility of simple signs is postulate of determinateness of sense
>
> 3.24   proposition in which there is talk of complex, if this does not exist, becomes not nonsense but simply false; combination of symbols of complex in simple symbol expressed by definition
>
> 4.026   meaning of simple signs must be explained
>
> 4.24   name is a simple symbol
>
> 5.4541   solutions of logical problems must be simple, for they set standard of simplicity
>
> 5.553   Russell said that there were simple relationships between different numbers of things

Simplest [einfachst]

> 4.21   the simplest proposition, the elementary proposition, asserts subsistence of a prime fact
>
> 6.363   process of induction is that of assuming simplest law that will do
>
> 6.3631   there are no grounds for believing that the simplest will be the case

Simplest [das Einfachste]

> 5.5563   what is simplest in regard to ordinary language, and what we should give here, is not a likeness of truth but the complete truth itself

Snags (catches) [Haken]

> 5.511   logic can use special snags because these are connected in a network to great mirror

Space [Raum]. See also Locus; Logical space; Place   175

    1.13   derivative facts in logical space are world

    2.0121   impossible to think of spatial objects apart from space

    2.013   each thing is in space of possible prime facts

    2.0131   spatial object must lie in infinite space

    2.0251   space is a form of objects

    2.11   image presents state of affairs in logical space

    2.202   image represents a possible state of affairs in
             logical space

    3.032   co-ordinates of figure which contradicts laws of
             space cannot be given

    3.42   whole logical space given with locus is determined by
             proposition; proposition reaches through whole logical
             space

    4.463   tautology leaves all logical space to actuality; con-
             tradiction fills it and leaves no point to actuality

    6.3111   Kantian problem of right and left hand also exists in
             one-dimensional space; is solved in four-dimensional
             space

    6.3611   description of event in space needs support from
             another event

    6.4312   solution of riddle of life lies outside space and time

Spatial [räumlich]

    2.0121   we cannot think spatial objects apart from space

    2.0131   spatial object must lie in infinite space

    2.171   spatial image can image everything spatial

    2.182   not every image is spatial

    3.0321   prime fact could be presented spatially which contra-
             dicted laws of physics but not those of geometry

    3.1431   propositional sign made clear by imagining it as com-
             bined out of spatial objects, whose mutual spatial
             location then expresses sense of proposition

    4.0412   idealist explanation of spatial relations through
             spatial spectacles inadequate because it gives no
             multiplicity

Index to Terms

176   Spatial Point [Raumpunkt]. See also Point; Spot

2.0131 a spatial point is a place for an argument

Speak [sprechen]. See also Enunciate; Express; Say; Talk

7.   of that of which one cannot speak, one must be silent

Special [speziell]

5.454   in logic there cannot be a more general and a more
        special

5.511   special snags and manipulations are connected in
        infinitely fine network

5.554   statement of special forms would be wholly arbitrary

Spectacles [Brille]

4.412   idealist account of spatial spectacles is inadequate

Spoken Language [Lautsprache]

4.011   phonetic spelling appears not to be image of spoken
        language, at first sight

Spot [Fleck]

2.0131 spot in visual field must have color and color-space
        around it

* 4.063 black spot on white paper as image of concept of truth

* 6.341 black spots on white surface described with aid of net

6.35   spots in image are geometrical, yet nothing can be
        said geometrically about their form and position

Stand [stehen]

4.0311 one name stands for one thing, another name for
        another thing

4.014   phonograph record, musical thought, score, sound
        waves, stand to one another in imaging internal rela-
        tion as language stands to world

Standard (Eng.)

5.4541 solutions of logical problems set the standard of
        simplicity

Stand As Proxy For (stand for, deputize, represent) [vertreten]

2.131   elements in image stand as proxies for objects

3.22   name in proposition stands as proxy for object

3.221   signs stand as proxies for objects

Stand As Proxy For (stand for, deputize, represent) [vertreten]
    continued
    4.0312   possibility of propositions rests on signs' standing
              as proxies for objects; logical constants do not stand
              as proxies; nothing can stand as proxy for the logic
              of derivative facts

Stand For [vorstellen]
    ("Presents" would do as well here, though giving a slightly
    different meaning, and would comport better with vorstellende
    as "presenting." But there seems no obvious clue to the
    perspective from which Wittgenstein wishes to view this re-
    lationship. At any rate we should avoid confusing it with
    the "represent," darstellen, that the philosopher evidently
    intends to keep within strict bounds.)

    2.11   image stands for state of affairs, the subsistence
             and non-subsistence of prime facts

    2.15   that elements of image are related in definite way
             stands for similar relation of things

    4.031   whole proposition stands for the prime fact

Standpoint [Standpunkt]

    2.173   standpoint of image is its form of representation

State of Affairs (way things lie, situation, circumstances)
    [Sachlage]
    (We have used "state of affairs" as a loose rendering of a
    virtually untranslatable - and, in Wittgenstein, highly
    important - word)

    2.0121   for a thing which could subsist of itself, subse-
              quently to be fitted to some state of affairs would
              seem accidental

    2.0122   thing is independent if it can occur in all possible
              states of affairs

    2.014   objects contain possibility of all states of affairs

    2.11   image presents state of affairs in logical space

    2.202   possible state of affairs in logical space is what
             the image images

    2.203   image contains possibility of state of affairs

    3.02   possibility of state of affairs is contained in the
             thought

    3.11   perceptible sign of proposition used as projection of
             possible state of affairs

    3.144   state of affairs can be described, not named

Index to Terms

Structure [Struktur]. See also Construction; Form

2.032   structure of prime fact is way objects hang together in it

2.033   form of objects is possibility of structure of facts

2.034   structure of derivative fact consists of structures of prime facts

2.15   connection of elements of image is its structure

4.014   to language and world, logical structure is common

4.1211   if two propositions contradict each other, this shows from their structure

4.122   property of structure is called "internal property," relation of structures, "internal relation"

5.13   that one proposition follows from others is perceived from structure of propositions

5.2   structures of propositions stand in internal relations

5.22   operation is expression of relation between structures of its result and its bases

6.12   for propositions bound up in definite way to give tautology, they must have definite properties of structure

6.3751   logical structure of color excludes possibility of two colors in one locus

Study [Studium]. See also Investigation

4.1121   Wittgenstein's study of sign-language corresponds to study of thought-processes

Sub specie aeterni

6.45   contemplation of world sub specie aeterni is its contemplation as a limited whole

Subject [Subjekt]

4.1274   one cannot ask whether there are unanalyzable subject-predicate propositions

5.5421   subject as conceived in contemporary superficial psychology is a nonentity

5.631   there is no thinking, presenting subject

5.632   subject limits the world

5.633   metaphysical subject is nowhere in the world

5.641   philosophical I is the metaphysical subject

Subsistence (existence) [das Bestehen] continued

4.21   elementary proposition asserts subsistence of a prime
        fact

4.27   number of possibilities of subsistence of prime facts,
        mathematically expressed; it is possible for all com-
        binations of prime facts to subsist, and the others
        not

4.3   truth-possibilities of elementary propositions mean
        possibilities of the subsistence and non-subsistence
        of prime facts

Subsistent (existent) [das Bestehende]

2.027   the fixed, the subsistent, and the object are one

2.0271 the object is the subsistent, the configuration is
        the changing

2.04   totality of subsistent prime facts is world

2.05   totality of subsistent prime facts determines which
        prime facts do not subsist

Substance [Substanz]

2.021   objects form substance of world

2.0211 sense of proposition would depend on truth of another
        proposition if world lacked substance

2.0231 substance can determine form only, not material
        properties

2.024   substance exists independently of what is the case

2.025   substance is form and content

4.463   proposition, image, and model are like space limited
        by solid substance, leaving place for a body

Substitutability [Ersetzbarkeit]

6.24   equations express substitutability of two expressions

Substitution [Substitution]

6.24   mathematics arrives at equations by method of sub-
        stitution

Successive [successiv]

6.001   every proposition the result of successive applica-
        tions of operation to elementary proposition

	3.321	two different symbols can have same sign in common, then designate differently
	3.323	a word designating in different ways belongs to different symbols
	3.325	to avoid errors we must not apply same sign in different symbols
	3.326	to recognize symbol in the sign we consider sense-bearing use
	3.341	essential in symbol is what symbols expressing identical sense have in common
	3.3411	proper name is what all symbols which designate an object have in common
	3.344	what designates in symbol is what is common to all symbols by which it can be replaced
	4.216	expression of formal property is a feature of certain symbols
	4.24	names are simple symbols
	4.465	essence of symbol cannot be altered without altering the sense
	4.4661	relations of signs in tautology or contradiction are unessential to symbol
	4.5	every possible sense can be expressed by symbol according to general form of proposition
	5.1311	that we can infer one proposition from another shows that generality is present in first symbol
	5.473	"Socrates is identical" is nonsensical because we have not made some arbitrary determination for "identical," not because symbol is impermissible
*	5.513	what is common to all symbols which assert p and q
	5.514	rules for constructing propositions are equivalent to symbols
	5.515	symbols must show that what are united by "v," etc., are propositions
	5.525	precedent for possibility of state of affairs to which one appeals must lie in symbol
	5.5261	composite symbol has something in common with other symbols
	5.555	where we build symbols according to system, latter is logically important

-T-

Tautology [Tautologie] continued

5.525   certainty of state of affairs is expressed by tautology

6.1   propositions of logic are tautologies

6.12   that propositions of logic are tautologies shows logical properties of language and world; constituents of tautology must have definite properties of structure

6.1201 propositions united to give tautology illustrate their structure as contradictions, etc.

6.1202 contradictions equally useful with tautologies to show properties of structure of propositions

* 6.1203 intuitive method for recognizing tautologies given

6.1221 if p and q give tautology in union, then q follows from p

6.124   that there are tautologies shows something about the world

6.126   proof of logical propositions consists in generating them out of tautologies

6.1262 proof in logic only an expedient for recognizing tautologies

6.127   each tautology shows that it is one

6.22   tautologies show about logic of world what equations show in mathematics

6.3751 logical product of two elementary propositions cannot be a tautology

Temporal [zeitlich]. See also Eternity; Time; Timelessness

2.0121 temporal object cannot be thought of apart from time

6.3611 comparison of temporal procedure possible through support of another procedure

6.4312 temporal immortality is no answer to riddle of life

Temporal Duration [Zeitdauer]

6.4311 eternity not necessarily understood is infinite temporal duration

Term. See Member

Thing [Ding] continued

4.063   proposition without sense signifies no thing (truth-
         value) whose properties are called "true" or "false"

4.1272   "thing" is rightly expressed in ideography by variable
         name x

4.243   whether we can understand two names without knowing if
         they designate same or different things

5.5301   proposition (x):fx ⊃ x = a says that only a satisfies
         a certain function f, and not that only such things
         satisfy function f which have a certain relation to a

5.5303   to say of two things that they are identical is non-
         sense; to say of one thing that it is identical is to
         say nothing

5.5351   when speaking of proto-image (proposition, thing,
         etc.), there is temptation to use expressions like
         a = a etc.

* 5.5352 defects in notation for "there are no things"

* 5.553   Russell and simple relations between different numbers
           of things

5.634   there is no a priori order of things

6.1231   to be general is only to be accidentally valid for all
         things

6.1263   proofs of logical and of sense-bearing propositions
         are different things

Think [denken]

2.0121   impossible to think of object apart from possibility
         of its union with others

2.013   we can think of space of possible prime facts as
         empty, but not of thing without space

3.02   thought contains possibility of state of affairs which
         it thinks

3.03   we cannot think anything unlogical, or unlogically

4.01   proposition a model of actuality as we think it is

5.61   we cannot say what we cannot think

5.631   no thinking, presenting subject exists

Thinkable [denkbar]

3.001   "a prime fact is thinkable," means we can image it

3.02   what is thinkable is also possible

Thought [Gedanke] continued

3.2   thoughts can be expressed in proposition so that ob-
         jects of thoughts correspond to elements of proposi-
         tional sign

3.5   the thought is the applied, thought-of, propositional
         sign

4.   the thought is the significant proposition

4.002   the thought is clothed by language

4.014   musical thought stands to phonograph record, etc., as
         language stands to world

4.0312   that logical constants do not represent is Wittgen-
         stein's fundamental thought

4.112   purpose of philosophy is logical clarification of
         thoughts

4.1121   Wittgenstein's study of sign-language is like study
         of thought-processes

6.21   propositions of mathematics express no thoughts

6.422   first thought in setting up ethical law of form "Thou
         shalt . . ." is, "What if I do not do it?"

Tied [verknüpfen]

2.1511   image is tied to actuality

6.12   that logic's constituents so tied give a tautology
         characterizes logic of world's constituents

Time [Zeit]

2.0121   temporal object cannot be thought of apart from time

2.0251   time is a form of objects

6.3611   there is no passage of time, hence no process can be
         compared with it

6.3751   particle cannot have two velocities at same time

6.4312   solution of riddle of life in space and time lies
         outside these

Timelessness [Unzeitlichkeit]

6.4311   if eternity means timelessness, to live in present is
         to live eternally

Tone [Ton]

2.031   a tone must have a pitch, as a spot must have a color
         space round it

Transition [Übergang]

    6.01   general form of transition from one proposition to
               another given

Translate [übersetzen]

    4.025   in translation of one language into another, one does
               not translate propositions but only their constitu-
               ents; dictionary translates substantives, adverbs,
               conjunctions, etc., all alike

    4.243   impossible not to be able to translate English and
               German words of like meaning into one another

Translation [Übersetzung]

    3.343   definitions are rules of translation

 * 4.0141   translation of the score into language of phonograph
               record

 * 4.025   translation of one language into another, using con-
               stituents of propositions

Treat [handeln]

    2.0121   logic treats of every possibility

    3.24   proposition which treats of complex stands in internal
               relation to proposition about its constituent

    3.317   fixing of values of propositional variable treats only
               with symbols, and not their meaning

    4.011   proposition does not at first appear to be image of
               actuality which it treats

    4.025   dictionary treats alike substantives, adjectives, and
               conjunctions

    4.122   existence of internal properties and relations shows
               itself in propositions which represent prime facts and
               treat of the objects

    5.44   proposition ~~p does not treat of denial as object

    5.542   in "A says p" we treat no co-ordination of derivative
               fact and object

    5.641   philosophical I is not what psychology treats of, but
               the metaphysical subject

    6.124   logical propositions "treat" of nothing

    6.35   laws, like proposition of causation, treat of net and
               not of what net describes

4.43   agreement of proposition with truth-possibilities of
          elementary propositions expressed by co-ordination
          with T in schemata

4.431   expression of agreement and disagreement with truth-
          possibilities of elementary propositions expresses
          truth-conditions of the proposition

4.44   sign arising from co-ordination of "true" in schemata
          with truth-possibilities is a propositional sign

4.442   if sequence of truth-possibilities is fixed in
          schemata last column becomes expression of truth-
          conditions

4.45   groups of truth-conditions which belong to truth-
          possibilities of number of elementary propositions
          can be ordered in series

4.46   propositions true for all truth-possibilities of its
          elementary propositions is tautology; proposition
          false for all its truth-possibilities is contradiction

5.101   truth-possibilities of proposition's truth-arguments
          are called its truth-grounds

Truth-value [Wahrheitswert]

4.063   proposition without sense designates no thing (truth-
          value) whose properties are "true" or "false"

Type (Eng.)

5.252   only as result of operation can be its own basis is
          progress from type to type in hierarchy of Russell and
          Whitehead possible

6.123   Russell mistaken in supposing special laws of contra-
          diction for each propositional type

-U-

Unanalyzed [unanalysiert]

5.5562   everyone knows that there must be elementary proposi-
          tions who understands propositions in unanalyzed form

Understand [verstehen]

4.003   most questions and propositions of philosophers rest
          on this, that we do not understand logic of language

4.016   to understand essence of proposition think of hiero-
          glyphic writing

Unessential [unwesentlich]

    4.1121   study of thought-processes got entangled in unessential psychological investigations

Ungeneralized [unverallgemeinert]

    5.5261   elements in generalized as well as ungeneralized propositions stand independently in designating relations to world

Unhappy Ones [die Unglücklichen]

    6.43   world of happy is different from that of unhappy ones

Union (combination, connection) [Verbindung]. See also Binding; Combination
(The word "unity" would do as well here, though it is not simple oneness that is meant. Wittgenstein uses Einheit only once or twice in the Tractatus, and then in a sense best rendered "unit.")

    2.01   a prime fact is a union of objects (entities, things)

    2.0121   possibility of object apart from union with others is unthinkable

    4.221   immediate elementary propositions are names in union; the question arises, how propositional union comes about

    4.466   to a logical union of signs corresponds one of meanings; no union of signs true for all cases is possible; to no logical union corresponds no union of objects; tautology and contradiction the limiting case of unions of signs

    5.451   fundamental concept must be introduced in all unions in which it occurs at all

    5.521   generality introduced in union with logical product or logical sum by Frege and Russell

    6.1201   union of p and ~p in the tautology

* 6.1203   union of true and false in bracket notation

    6.1221   if p and q give a tautology in union of p ⊃ q, it is clear that q follows from p

    6.124   union of logical propositions with world presupposes that names have meaning and propositions have sense

Unite (connect) [verbinden]

    4.0311   a name stands for one thing and another for another thing, and they are united together

    6.12   that propositions are united in tautology shows they possess definite structural properties

Index to Terms

202 Unite (connect) [verbinden] continued

6.121 propositions of logic unite propositions into those
saying nothing

6.1221 that q follows from (p ⊃ q) · p can be seen from propositions or by uniting propositions in right way and
showing this is tautology

6.232 what is essential in equation is that it is not necessary to show that expressions it unites have same
meaning

United (connected) [verbunden]

4.4661 signs are also united in tautology and contradiction,
but these relations are meaningless

5.515 that propositions are what are united by v, etc., must
emerge in our symbols

6.1201 propositions united in definite ways to show properties of their structures

Universality. See Generality

Unlogical [unlogisch]

3.303 we can think nothing unlogical

Unnecessary [unnötig]

5.47321 Occam's Razor says that unnecessary signs are without
meaning

Unsayable (unspeakable) [Unsagbar]

4.115 philosophy will mean the unsayable by clearly representing the Sayable

Unstable [das Unbeständige]

2.0271 the configuration of objects is the unstable

Unthinkable [undenkbar]

4.123 property is internal if it is unthinkable that its
object does not possess it

Use [Gebrauch]

3.326 to recognize symbol in sign, consider its sense-
bearing use

4.123 shifting use of "object" corresponds to that of
"property," or "relation"

5.252 Russell and Whitehead make use of possibility of
progress from type to type

3.328   sense of Occam's Razor: if a sign is not used it is meaningless

4.1272   nonsense arises when words like "object" are used not as variable names but as proper-concept words

4.241   that two signs are used with one meaning is expressed by putting between them sign of identity

-V-

Validity. See General Validity

Value [Wert]

Foreword: value of Tractatus lies in expression and truth of its thoughts

3.313   expression represented by variable whose values are propositions

3.315   if constituent of proposition is changed into variable, there is a class of propositions which are its values

3.316   what values propositional variable can assume is fixed; fixing of values is the variable

3.317   fixing of values of propositional variable is declaration of propositions whose common mark the variable is

4.127   values of proposition variable designating formal concept designate objects which fall under concept

4.1271   constant form of variable can be conceived as a forward property of values

5.501   values of variable in notation must be determined

* 5.502   notation for negation of collected values of a propositional variable given

5.51   if propositional variable has one value, negation of that variable negates that value; if two values, it negates both

* 5.52   values of ξ assigned

6.4   all propositions are equal in value

6.41   value must lie outside happening and being-so

Variable [Variable] continued

* 5.501   notational use of variable ($\bar{\xi}$) explained; values of
            variable must be determined

Velocities [Geschwindigkeiten]

6.3751   a particle cannot have two velocities

Verb [Verbum]

3.323   in ordinary language "to exist" appears as intransi-
          tive verb like "to go"

4.063   what "is true" already contains verb of proposition

Vicious Circle [circulus vitiosus]

4.1273   Frege and Russell's notion of the ideographic symbols
          for "b is a successor of a" contains a vicious circle

Visual Field [Gesichtsfeld]

2.0131   spot in visual field must have color

5.633   visual field and eye are like world and subject; from
          nothing in visual field can seeing eye be inferred

5.6331   visual field has no form which includes eye

6.3751   for two colors to be in one place in visual field is
          impossible, even logically impossible; assertion that
          a point in visual field has two different colors at
          same time

6.4311   endlessness of life like limitlessness of visual field

-W-

Weather [Wetter]

4.461   I know nothing about the weather in knowing that it
          rains or does not rain

Weltanschauung (Ger.)

6.371   illusion at basis of modern Weltanschauung that laws
          of nature explain phenomena

What [Was]

5.552   logic is before the how, not before the what

208   World [Welt]

	4.462	conditions of agreement with world cancel in tautology
	5.123	if God creates world in which certain propositions are true, he also creates world of their objects and in which following propositions are true
	5.4711	to supply essence of proposition means to give essence of all description, thus essence of world
	5.511	logic is world-mirroring
	5.526	world can be completely described by completely generalized propositions
	5.5261	parts of propositions have independent designating relations to world
	5.5262	general structure of world is altered by truth or falsity of propositions
	5.551	logical problems need not be solved by looking at world
*	5.5521	whether logic could exist without world
	5.6	limits of my language are limits of my world
	5.61	limits of world are also limits of logic; to exclude possibilities logic would have to get outside limits of world
	5.62	world is my world, as limits of my language are limits of world
	5.621	world and life are one
	5.63	I am my world
*	5.631	contents of book "The World as I Found It" considered
	5.632	subject limits world
	5.633	metaphysical subject is nowhere in world
	5.641	philosophical I is not a part of world
	6.12	formal properties of world shown in propositions of logic being tautologies
	6.1233	logic is not concerned with whether our world is of a sort to make propositions like Axiom of Reducibility valid
	6.124	logical propositions represent scaffolding of world
	6.13	logic is mirror image of world

Writing [Schrift]   211

     3.143   customary form of expression of writing conceals that
                propositional sign is derivative fact

Written Sign [Schriftzeichen]

     3.11   written sign used as projection of state of affairs

     3.1431 we may image propositional sign to be made of spatial
                objects instead of written signs

-X-

"X"

     4.1272 "x" as a variable name

-Y-

Yes [ja]

     4.023   actuality fixed by the proposition with respect to
                yes or no

-Z-

Zero [Null]

   * 4.1272 expressions like "there is only one zero" are nonsense

Zero-method. <u>See</u> Method

GERMAN-ENGLISH WORDLIST

This is simply to offer indications of where to look among our English entries. In general, proper names, Latin expressions, and English words appearing in the original German text are not included here.

-A-

A denkt p - A thinks p
A sagt p - A says p
abbilden - image
Abbildend - imaging
Abbildung - imaging
Aberglaube - superstition
abgebildet - imaged
abgrenzen - delimit
abhängen - depend
Ablauf - passage
Abmachungen - stipulations
Abschluss - conclusion
abstrakt - abstract
Abzeichen - distinguishing mark
Addition - addition
Additionszeichen - addition sign
Aesthetik - aesthetics
Ähnlichkeit - similarity
alle - all
allgemein - general
allgemeine Form - general form
allgemeiner Satz - general proposition
allgemeines Glied - general member
Allgemeingültigkeit - general validity
Allgemeinheit - generality
Allgemeinheitbezeichnung - designation of generality
allumfassend - all-embracing
alt - old
Alten - ancients
analog - analogous
Analoge - analogue
Analyse - analysis
analysiert - analyzed
analytisch - analytic
Angabe - declaration

angelegt - laid against
angenehm - pleasant
angewandt - applied
Annahme - assumption
annehmen - assume
anschaulich - intuitive
Anschauung - intuition
Ansehen - inspection
Antwort - answer
Anwendung - application
Anzahl - number
Anzeichen - symptom
Apparat - apparatus
Äquivalent - equivalent
Argument - argument
Argumentstelle - place for an argument
Arithmetik - arithmetic
artikuliert - articulated
Assymetrie - assymetry
auffassen - conceive, conceived
Aufgabe - task
aufhören - cease
Auflösung - dissolution, resolution
Augschluss - information
Aufstellen - setting up
aufweisen - exhibit
Aufzählung - enumeration
Auge - eye
Ausdruck - expression
ausdrücken - express
Ausdrucksform - form of expression
Ausdrucksweise - means of expression
auseinanderlegen - take apart
ausgedrückt - expressed
ausgezeichnet - pre-eminent
Aussage - assertion
aussagen - assert
aussprechen - enunciate
Axiome - axioms

213

214   -B-

Basen - bases
Bau - construction
bauen - construct
bedeuten - mean
Bedeutung - meaning
bedeutungslos - meaningless
bedeutungsvoll - meaningful
Bedingung - condition
Behelf - expedient
begrenzen - delimit
Begriff - concept
Begriffsschrift - ideography
Begriffswort - concept-word
Begründung - foundation
bejahen - affirm
Bejahung - affirmation
bekleidet - clothed
benennen - named
berechnen - calculate
Bereich - scope
berühren - touch
beschreiben - describe
Beschreibung - description
beschrieben - described
Bestandteil - constituent
bestehen - consist, subsist
Bestehen - subsistence
bestehend - subsistent
bestimmen - determine
bestimmt - determinate, determined
Bestimmtheit - determinateness
Bestimmung - determination
bestreitbar - disputable
Beurteilung - judgment
Beweis - proof
beweisen - prove
bezeichnen - designate
bezeichnend - designating
Bezeichnete - (the) designated
Bezeichnung - designation
Bezeichnungsweise - manner of
   designating
Beziehung - relation
Bild - image
Bildelement - image-element
bilden - form, image
Bildhaftigkeit - imagery
blau - blue
böse - evil
Brille - spectacles
Buch - book
Buchstaben - letters
Buchstabenschrift - alphabetic
   writing

              -C-

Charakter - character

charkterisieren - characterize
charakteristisch - characteristic

              -D-

darstellen - represent
Darstellung - representation
Definieren - defining
Definition - definition
definitiv - definitive
demonstrieren - demonstrate
denkbar - thinkable
denken - think
Denken - thinking
Dimensionen - dimensions
Ding - thing
Drucke - printing
Dualismus - dualism
dynamisch - dynamic

              -E-

Eben - plane
Eigenschaft - property
Eigenschaftswort - adjective
eigentlich - proper, properly
eigentlicher Begriff - proper
   concept
einfach - simple
einfachst - simplest
Einfachste - simplest
Einführung - introduction
Einklang - accord
Einleuchten - evidence, self-
   evidence
Einsichten - insights
Element - element
Elementarsatz - elementary proposition
empfinden - perceive
empirisch - empirical
endlich - finite
enthalten - contain, contained
enthaltend - containing
entnehmen - extract
entsprechen - correspond
entstehen - arise
entwerfen - frame
Ereignis - event
Erfahrung - experience
Erforschung - investigation
Erhaltungsgesetz - Law of Conservation
erläutern - elucidate
Erläuterungen - elucidations
erlebt - survived
erkennen - recognize
Erkennen - recognition
Erkenntnistheorie - epistemology

erklärt - clarified
Erklärung - clarification
Ermanglung - default
erschaffen - create
Erscheinungen - appearances
erschliessen - disclosed
Ersetzbarkeit - substitutability
ersetzt - replaced
Ethik - ethics
ethisch - ethical
Existenz - existence
existieren - exist
Experiment - experiment
Exponent - exponent
extern - external
ewig - eternal
Ewigkeit - eternity

-F-

Fähigkeit - capacity
Faktum - fact
Fall - case
falsch - false
Farbe - color
Farbenraum - color-space
färbig - colored
Färbigkeit - coloredness
farblos - colorless
Fehler - mistake
fest - fixed, solid
festgesetzt - fixed
festlegen - establish
Festsetzung - fixing
feststellen - establish
Figur - figure
fixiert - fixed
Fläche - surface
Fleck - spot
Folgen - effects
folgen - follow
folgenschwer - consequential
folgern - deduce
Folgern - inference
Folgesätze - consequent propositions
fordern - postulate
Forderung - postulate
Form - form
Form der Abbildung - form of
imaging
Form der Darstellung - form of
representation
Form der Wirklichkeit - form of
actuality
formal - formal
formaler Begriff - formal concept
formale Eigenschaft - formal
property
Formenreihe - formal series
Formgebung - fashioning
fortleben - survival

Fortschreiten - progress
Frage - question
fragen - question
Funktion - function
Fühler - feelers

-G-

Gang - movement
ganz - whole, wholly
Ganze - (the) whole
Gattungsname - generic name
Gebäude - building
Gebiet - realm
Gebilde - pattern
gebildet - formed
Gebrauch - use
gebraucht - used
gedacht - thought
Gedanke - thought
Gefühl - feeling
Gegenstand - object
Gegenwart - present
gegenwärtig - present
gegliedert - jointed
gelöst - solved
gemein - common
gemeinsam - common
Gemisch - mixture
Geometrie - geometry
geometrisch - geometrical
Gerüst - scaffolding
gesagt - said
gesamt - total
Gesamtheit - totality
geschehen - happen
Geschehen - happening
Geschwindigkeiten - velocities
Gesetz - law
Gesetz der Kleinsten Wirkung - Law
of Least Action
Gesetz des Widerspruchs - Law of
Contradiction
gesetzmässig - conforming to law
Gesetzmässigkeit - conformity to
law
Gesicht - fact
Gesichtsfeld - visual field
gewiss - certain
Gewissheit - certainty
glauben - believe
gleichbedeutend - like in meaning
Gleichheit - sameness
Gleichheitszeichen - sign of
equality
Gleichnis - likeness
Gleichung - equation
gleichwertig - equal in value
Glied - member
Glücklichen - happy (ones)
Gott - God
Grad - degree

216   Gradation - gradation
Grammophonplatte - phonograph record
Grammatik - grammar
Grenze - limit
grenzen - limit
grenzenlos - limitless
Grenzfall - limiting case
grün - green
Grund - ground
Grundbegriff - fundamental concept
Grundgedanke - fundamental thought
Grundgesetz - fundamental law
grundlegend - fundamental
Grundoperation - fundamental operation
Gruppe - group
Gute - good

-H-

Haken - snags
Hand - hand
handeln - treat
Handlung - action
Handschuh - glove
hängen - hang
herausheben - distinguish
hervorheben - distinguish
Hierarchie - hierarchy
Hieroglyphenschrift - hieroglyphic writing
Höheres - higher
Hypothese - hypothesis
hypothetisch - hypothetically

-I-

ich - I
Idee - idea
Idealist - Idealist
identisch - identical
Index - index
Induktion - induction
Inhalt - content
intern - internal
Interpunktion - punctuation
Irrtum - error

-J-

ja - yes

-K-

Kardinalzahlen - cardinal numbers
Kausalität - causality
Kausalitätsgesetz - causal law
Kausalnexus - causal nexus
kennen - cognize
Kette - chain
Klammern - brackets
klar - clear
klar - clearly
Klärung - clarification
Klarwerden - clarifying
Klasse - class
Klassifikation - classification
kollidieren - collide
Kombination - combination
komplex - complex
Komplex - complex
kompliziert - complicated
kennzeichnen - mark
Konfiguration - configuration
konkret - concrete
konstant - constant
Konstante - constant
konstruieren - construct
konstruiert - constructed
Konstruktion - construction
Kontinuität - continuity
Kontradiktion - contradiction
kontradiktorisch - contradictory
Koordinaten - co-ordinates
Koordination - co-ordination
koordiniert - co-ordinated
Kopula - copula
Körper - body

-L-

Lage - position
Lautzeichen - sound-sign
Lautsprache - spoken language
Lautzeichenschrift - phonetic spelling
Leben - life
Lebend - living
leer - empty
Lehre - doctrine
Leib - body
Leiter - ladder
Logik - logic
logisch - logical, logically
Lohn - reward
Lösung - solution

-M-

machen - make
Manipulation - manipulation
Mannigfaltigkeit - multiplicity
Masstab - measuring stick
materiell - material
Mathematik - mathematics
mathematisch - mathematical
Mechanik - mechanics
mechanisch - mechanical
Mensch - man
menschlich - human
Merkmal - mark
metaphysisch - metaphysical
Methode - method
Mikrokosmos - Microcosm
Minimum Gesetze - minimum-laws
mitteilen - impart
Mittelpunkt - center
Modell - model
möglich - possible
Möglichkeit - possibility
Monismus - Monism
Musik - music
musikalisch - musical
Mystische - mystical

-O-

Objekt - object
Operation - operation
Ordnung - order
Organismus - organism
Ort - locus

-P-

Papier - paper
Paradox - paradox
Pfeile - arrows
Phänomen - phenomenon
Philosophen - philosophers
Philosophie - philosophy
philosophisch - philosophic
Physik - physics
physikalisch - physical
positiv - positive
Prädikat - predicate
präjudiziert - prejudged
praktisch - practical
Prinzip - principle
Problem - problem
Produkt - product
Projektion - projection
projektiv - projective
Prozess - process
Psychologie - psychology
psychologisch - psychological
Punkt - point

-N-

Nachfolger - successor
Name - name
Natur - nature
Naturerscheinungen - natural
   phenomena
Naturgesetz - Law of Nature
Naturwissenschaft - natural
   science
Negation - negation
negativ - negative
Negativ - negative
nein - no
nennen - name
Netz - net
Netzwerk - network
neu - new
Neuheit - novelty
Nichtbestehen - non-subsistence
nichtpsychologisch - non-psycho-
   logical
Nichtsatz - non-proposition
Nichtübereinstimmung - disagree-
   ment
Notation - notation
Notenschrift - score
nötig - necessary
notwendig - necessary
Notwendigkeit - necessity

-R-

Rätsel - riddle
Raum - space
räumlich - spatial
Raumpunkt - spatial point
Realismus - realism
Realität - reality
Rechnung - calculation
Rede - talk
reden - talk
Regel - rule
reichen - reach
Reihe - series
Reihenfolge - serial order
Relation - relationship
Resultat - result
Richtigkeit - correctness
Rolle - role

-S-

Sachen - entities
Sachlage - state of affairs
Sachverhalt - prime fact
sagbar - (the) sayable
sagen - say
sämtliche - collective
Satz - proposition
Satz vom Grunde - principle of
    causation
Satzbestandteile - propositional
    constituents
Satzform - propositional form
Satzgefüge - propositional struc-
    ture
Satzvariable - propositional
    variable
Satzverband - propositional union
Satzzeichen - propositional sign
Schallwellen - sound waves
Scheinbegriff - illusory concept
Scheinbeziehung - illusory rela-
    tion
Scheinsatz - illusory proposition
Scheinungen - appearances
Schema - schema
Schicksal - fate
schliessen - infer
Schliessen - inference
Schluss - conclusion, inference
Schöne - beautiful
Schrift - writing
Schriftzeichen - written sign
schweigen - (be) silent
Seele - soul
sehen - see
selbständig - independently, self-
    dependent
Selbständigkeit - independence
Sinn - sense
sinnlich - sensible, sensibly
sinnlos - senseless
sinnvoll - sense-bearing
skeptizismus - scepticism
So-Sein - being-so
Solipsismus - solipsism
Sonne - sun
speziell - special
Spiegel - mirror
Spiegelbild - mirror image
spiegeln - mirror
spiegelt - mirrored
Spielraum - elbowroom
Sprache - language
Sprachkritik - critique of
    language
Sprachlogik - logic of language
sprechen - speak
Standpunkt - standpoint
stehen - stand
Stelle - place
stellen - place
stimmen - agree

Stimmen - agreement
Strafe - punishment
Struktur - structure
Studium - study
Subjekt - subject
Substanz - substance
Substitution - substitution
successiv - successive
Summe - sum
Symbol - symbol
Symbolik - symbolism
Symbolismus - symbolism
symmetrisch - symmetrical
syntaktisch - syntactic
Syntax - syntax
System - system

                    -T-

Tastsinn - touch
Tätigkeit - activity
Tatsache - derivative fact
tatsächlich - factually
Täuschung - illusion
Tautologie - tautology
tautologisch - tautological
Teil - part
Teilchen - particle
Thema - theme
Theorie - theory
Tisch - table
Tod - death
Ton - tone
Träger - bearer
transcendental - transcendental

                    -U-

Übereinkunft - agreement
Übereinstimmung - agreement
Übergang - transition
Überraschungen - surprises
übersetzen - translate
Übersetzung - translation
Überwinden - surmount
Umgangssprache - colloquial lan-
    guage
Umstände - circumstances
unabhängig - independent
unanalysiert - unanalyzed
Unaussprechliches - inenunciable
Unbeständige - unstable
Unbestimmtheit - indefiniteness
undenkbar - unthinkable
Unding - nonentity
unendlich - infinite
Unglückliche - unhappy ones
unlogisch - unlogical
unmöglich - impossible

Unmöglichkeit - impossibility
Unregelmässigkeiten - irregularities
Unsagbar - (the) unsayable
Unselbständigkeit - dependence
Unsinn - nonsense
unsinnig - nonsensical
Unsinnigkeit - nonsensicality
Unsterblichkeit - immortality
unterschieden - differentiated
Untersuchungen - investigations
unverallgemeinert - ungeneralized
unwesentlich - unessential
Unzeitlichkeit - timelessness
Urbild - proto-image
Ursache - cause
urteilen - judge
Urteilsstrich - assertion sign
Urzeichen - proto-sign

-V-

variabel - variable
Variable - variable
verallgemeinern - generalize
Verallgemeinerung - generalization
Verband - binding
verbinden - unite
Verbindung - union
Verbum - verb
verbunden - united
verbürgen - assure
vergleichen - compare
Vergleichsobjekt - object for comparison
verhalten - related
Verkettung - concatenation
verkleiden - clothe
verknüpfen - tie
Verlauf - passage
verneinen - deny
Verneinung - denial
verschieden - differ, different
Verschiedenheit - difference
verschlucken - conceal
Verschwinden - vanishing
verstanden - understood
verständigen - interpret
Verständnis - understanding
verstehen - understand
Versuch - attempt, experiment
vertreten - stand as proxies for
Verwechslung - confusion
Verwendung - application
vollständig - complete, completely
voraussehen - foresee
Vorbereitung - preliminary
Vorgang - procedure
vorkommen - occur
Vorkommen - occurrence

vorstellen - stand for   219
vorstellend - presenting

-W-

wahr - true
wahr oder falsch - true or false
Wahrheit - truth
Wahrheit oder Falschheit - truth or falsity
Wahrheitsargument - truth-argument
Wahrheitsbedingung - truth-condition
Wahrheitsbegriff - truth-concept
Wahrheitsfunktion - truth-function
Wahrheitsgründe - truth-grounds
Wahrheitskombination - truth-combination
Wahrheitsmöglichkeiten - truth-possibilities
Wahrheitsoperationen - truth-operations
Wahrheitswert - truth-value
wahrnehmbar - perceptible
wahrnehmen - perceive
wahrscheinlich - probable
Wahrscheinlichkeit - probability
Wahrscheinlichkeitslehre - probability theory
Wahrscheinlichkeitssatz - probability proposition
Was - what
wechselnd - altering
weisen - display
Welt - world
Weltanschauung
Weltbeschreibung - world description
Werk - work
Wert - value
Wesen - essence
wesentlich - essential, essentially
Wetter - weather
widersprechen - contradict
Widerspruch - contradiction
Wie - how
willkürlich - arbitrary, arbitrarily
Wille - will
Willensfreiheit - freedom of will
wirklich - actual, actually
Wirklichkeit - actuality
Wirkung - action
Wissen - knowledge
Wissenschaft - science
wissenschaftlich - scientific
Wollen - willing
Wort - word
Würfel - cube

220   -Z-

Zahl - number
Zahlbegriff - number concept
Zahlengleichheit - numerical
  equality
Zahlenreihe - number series
Zahlenzeichen - numerical sign
zahllos - numerical
zeichen - sign
Zeichenregel - sign rule
Zeichensprache - sign-language
Zeichenverbindung - sign-union
Zeigen - show
Zeit - time
Zeitdauer - temporal duration
zeitlich - temporal
zerfallen - break up
zergliedert - dismembered

zerlegen - divided
Zufall - accident
zufällig - accidental
zufälligerweise - accidentally
Zug - feature
Zukunft - future
zuordnen - co-ordinate
Zuordnungen - co-ordinations
zusammenfallen - coincide
Zusammenfassung - merging
zusammengesetzt - composite
Zusammengesetztheit - composite-
  ness
zusammengestellt - put together
Zusammenhang - coherence
zusammenhängen - cohere
Zusammensetzung - composition
Zwang - compulsion
Zweck - purpose
Zweifel - doubt

LOGISTIC SYMBOLS

We include those symbols which are used in any cognitive sense, or are in some way explained, defined, or related in a series to other symbols receiving such explanation.

3.1432	aRb	5.02	c as index
3.203	A	5.02	p as an argument
3.333	F(fx)	5.101	TTTT
3.333	φ(fx)		....
			FFFF
		5.12	p,q
4.012	$(\exists \varphi):F(\varphi\mu).\varphi\mu = f\mu$	5.1241	p,q
4.0411	(x).fx; Gen.fx; f(xg);	5.1311	p v q . ~p:⊃q
	(G,G).F(G,G)	5.1311	(x).fx ⊃ fa
4.002	p; ~p	5.132	p follows from a
4.063	p	5.1362	A knows that p is the
4.1211	fa; ga		case
4.1252	aRb	5.15	Trs:Tr
4.1252	aRb (∃x):aRx.xRb	5.151	Trs:Tr
	(∃x,y):aRx.xRy.yRb	5.152	probability 1/2
4.1272	variable name x	5.152	p follows from a
4.1272	(∃x,y)	5.154	probability 1/2
	$\aleph_0$ objects	5.2341	truth-function of p
4.1272	1, null.	5.242	p, q, r as variables
4.1273	aRb	5.2521	0'0'0'a
4.1273	aRx.xRb	5.2521	0''ξ applies to a
4.1273	(Ex,y):aRx.xRy.yRb	5.2522	0'a, 0'0a, ...
4.24	fx; φ(x,y)	5.2522	(a, x, 0'x)
4.24	p, q, r	5.254	~~p.~~p = p
4.241	=, a = b	5.31	p, q, r as non-elementary
4.241	Def.		propositions
4.242	a = b	5.42	v, ⊃, etc.
4.243	a = a	5.43	p, ~~p, ~~~p
4.27	$K_n = \sum_{\nu=0}^{n} \binom{n}{\nu}$	5.441	~(∃x).~fx
			(x).fx
4.31	p, q, r in TF combi-		(∃x).fx.x = a
	nation		fa
4.42	$\sum_{k=0}^{K_n} \binom{K_n}{k} = L_n$	5.451	~p
			~(p v q)
			(∃x).~fx
4.44	~p	5.46	p v q
4.442	table		~p (v~q)
		5.47	(∃x).fx.x = a
			fa
		5.5	(-----T) (ξ, ...)
		5.501	(ξ), ξ
		5.502	(-----T) (ξ, ...)
4.442	⊢	5.502	N(ξ)
4.442	(TTFT) (p,q)	5.51	N(ξ) = ~p
4.45	Ln groups of truth-		N(ξ) = ~p.~q
	conditions	5.512	~p ⊃p, ~~~p
4.4611	0 (in arithmetic)	5.513	q: pv~p

4.442

p	q	
T	T	T
F	T	T
T	F	
F	F	T

SELECTED BIBLIOGRAPHY

This is not a list of books one should read in order to understand the Tractatus - what would that list contain, anyway? - but
rather a selection of books and articles purporting to explain or
refute all or parts of that work. Certain biographical materials have
been included because they throw some light upon the period of the
composition of the Tractatus. There seems little need to list all
the published works of Wittgenstein himself, but only those that bear
directly upon the book on which we are concentrating; and we make
note of one or two manuscripts. The most interesting and informative
manuscript account of the life of the philosopher which we have seen
has not yet found its way into print.
Owing to our restrictions, this list will not contain, even if
it ought to, "the magnificent works of Frege and the writings of my
friend Mr. Bertrand Russell," nor the books of Hertz, Mauthner, and
others to whom reference is made in Tractatus. The list is printed
alphabetically by authors, without further subdivisions.

Anscombe, G. E. M. "Mr. Copi on Objects, Properties and Relations
in the Tractatus," Mind, Vol. LXVIII, No. 271 (July 1959),
p. 404.
A brief note, chiefly on the problems of aRb and mathematical
multiplicity.

_____. An Introduction to Wittgenstein's 'Tractatus.' London:
Hutchinson University Library, 1959.
The author has had two unusual advantages in the writing of this
book: personal association with Wittgenstein, and intimate
knowledge of virtually all his unpublished and published work.
The second advantage is the more important in this case, and
leads to an exposition of considerable exactness, though the
book is neither a complete account nor an elementary one.

Anscombe, G. E. M., R. Rhees, and G. H. von Wright. A note on
Costello's version of the "Notes on Logic," Journal of Philo-
sopy, Vol. LIV, No. 15 (July 18, 1957), p. 484.

Ayer, A. J. "Demonstration of the Impossibility of Metaphysics,"
Mind, Vol. XLII, No. 171 (July 1934), pp. 335-45.
Discussion of the problem partly in the light of Wittgenstein's
ladder.

Barone, F. "Ludwig Wittgenstein," Enciclopedia Filosofica, 1957.
A brief and useful summary.

Black, Max. Philosophical Analysis: A Collection of Essays.
Ithaca, New York: Cornell University Press, 1950.
The introduction by Black, contains some remarks on the influ-
ence of the Tractatus.

224   _____. "Some Problems Connected with Language," Proceedings of the
Aristotelian Society, Vol. XXXIX (1939), pp. 43-68.
This paper is reprinted as chapter 6, "Wittgenstein's Tractatus,"
pp. 199-201 in Black's Language and Philosophy (Ithaca, New
York: Cornell University Press.)

_____. The Nature of Mathematics. London: Kegan Paul, Trench, Trubner
and Co.; New York: Harcourt Brace and Co., 1933.
Contains a chapter of moderate value on Wittgenstein's mathematical views in the Tractatus.

Chadwick, J. A. "Logical Constants," Mind, Vol. XXXVI, No. 141
(January 1927), pp. 1-11.
Where it concerns the Tractatus, this article touches upon
tautology.

Copi, Irving M. "Objects, Properties and Relations in the Tractatus,"
Mind, Vol. LXVII, No. 266 (April 1958), pp. 145-65.
An elaborate article on several interrelated topics, including
the question of mathematical multiplicity.

Cranston, Maurice. "Ludwig Wittgenstein," World Review, August 1951,
pp. 21-24
A sympathetic sketch of Wittgenstein's life and some of his
characteristic opinions, early and late. The following issue of
the Review published a peremptory correction, by G. E. M. Anscombe, of some inaccuracies in the sketch.

Daitz, Edna. "The Picture Theory of Meaning," Mind, Vol. LXII,
No. 246 (April 1953), pp. 184-201.
Pictures, maps, and propositions in their correspondence to
things.

Daly, C. B. "New Light on Wittgenstein," in Philosophical Studies.
St. Patrick's College, Maynooth, Ireland, 1960.
This longish essay chiefly sums up the arguments in favor of
Wittgenstein's general approach, and touches upon some of his
chief contentions in the Tractatus. There is some light, but it
is hardly new.

Evans, Ellis. "Tractatus 3.1432," Mind, Vol. LXIV, No. 254 (April
1955), pp. 259-60.
Regarding aRb: answer to Edna Daitz.

_____. "About 'aRb,'" Mind, Vol. LXVIII, No. 272 (October 1959)
pp. 535-38.

Feibleman, James K. Inside the Great Mirror. The Hague: Martinus
Nijhoff.
The early portions of this book cover roughly the same ground
as does Urmson's, but at greater length and with more effort to
interpret the Tractatus in a new fashion. One might remark that
in Feibleman's hands the Tractatus becomes a representative
sample of philosophizing in the United States, say in the 1920s.

Geach, P. T. Review of the Tractatus Logico-Philosophicus in the
Italian translation by Gian Carlo Colombo, in The Philosophical
Review, Vol. LXVI, No. 4 (October 1957).
Even in a review as brief as this, Geach makes several valuable
points about the Tractatus and the terminological problems it
raises.

Hamburg, Carl. "Whereof One Cannot Speak," The Journal of Philosophy, Vol. L, No. 22 (October 22, 1953), pp. 662-64.
Tractatus 7. interpreted with no more than passing reference to 1.-6.54.

Harris, Errol E. Nature, Mind and Modern Science. London: George Allen & Unwin Ltd.; New York: The Macmillan Company, 1954.
An unfavorable estimate of many trends in the modern philosophy of science, with some attention to Wittgenstein.

Hawkins, D. J. B. Wittgenstein and the Cult of Language. London: Blackfriars Publications, 1957. The Aquinas Society of London: Aquinas Paper No. 27.
A relatively unsympathetic account, from a Thomistic standpoint.

Heller, Erich. "Ludwig Wittgenstein: Unphilosophical Notes," Encounter, Vol. XIII, no. 3 (September 1959).
An essay of more than ordinary literary and cultural sensitivity, which helps to give Wittgenstein his proper spirtual setting.

Hintikka, Jaakko. "On Wittgenstein's 'Solipsism,'" Mind, Vol. LXVII, No. 265 (January 1958), pp. 88-91.
Discussion of 5.62, and how this differs from the "other minds" problem of later analysts. Part of the essay turns upon a disputed translation.

Jørgensen, Jørgen. A Treatise of Formal Logic. London: Humphrey Milford, Oxford University Press, 1931, 3 vols.
Vols. I and III contain a number of references to the Tractatus, mainly in the context of what it means to be a logical system.

Kraft, Viktor. Der Wiener Kreis, der Urspring des Neopositivismus, ein Kapitel der jungsten Philosophiegeschichte. Wien: Springer-Verlag, 1950. Translated into English by Arthur Pap as The Vienna Circle. New York: Philosophical Library, 1953.
Inclines to accept the Tractatus as an early statement, rather than a variant, of Logical Postivism.

Langford, C. H. "On Propositions Belonging to Logic," Mind, Vol. XXXVI, No. 143 (July 1927), pp. 342-46.
A series of objections to Wittgenstein's theory of tautology.

Lieb, Irwin C. "Wittgenstein's Investigations," Review of Metaphysics, Vol. VIII, No. 1 (September 1954), pp. 125-43.
Relations between the Tractatus and Philosophical Investigations on certain salient points.

McTaggart, J. Ellis. "Propositions Applicable to Themselves," Mind, Vol. XXXII, No. 128 (October 1923), pp. 462-64.
Clarification of an alleged ambiguity in the Tractatus.

Malcolm, Norman. Ludwig Wittgenstein, A Memoir. London: Oxford University Press, 1958.
With a biographical sketch by Georg Henrik von Wright. The Malcolm essay is chiefly a personal reminiscence, containing many of Wittgenstein's letters, of the philosopher's last 15 years. That by von Wright is a short, balanced account of the man's whole life.

Selected Bibliography

226   Maslow, Alexander P. A Study of Ludwig Wittgenstein's Tractatus
      Logico-Philosophicus. University of California, Doctoral Dis-
      sertation, 1934.
      One of the earliest, most neglected, and most thorough works
      covering several, though not all, important aspects of the
      Tractatus. This work, in much the same form, has recently
      (1961) been published by tne University of California Press,
      under the same title.

      Moore, Willis. "Structure in Sentence and in Fact," Philosophy of
      Science, Vol. V, No. 1 (January 1938).
      A brief, insightful essay which does away with several erroneous
      interpretations of the likeness of image and fact alleged in the
      Tractatus.

      Palmer, H. "The Other Logical Constant," Mind, Vol. LXVII, No. 265
      (January 1958), pp. 50-59.
      A variety of linguistic topics considered in the light of cer-
      tain statements in the Tractatus, and a criticism of them.

      Plochmann, George Kimball. Review of G. E. M. Anscombe, An Intro-
      duction to Wittgenstein's Tractatus, in The Modern Schoolman,
      Vol. XXXVII (March 1960), pp. 242-46.

      Popper, Karl R. The Open Society and Its Enemies. Princeton, New
      Jersey: Princeton University Press, 1950.
      The author tilts at a good many giants, thinking them windmills.
      Wittgenstein fares better than Plato in this very long book, and
      that is all that can be said of the treatment of him.

      Ramsey, F. P. Foundations of Mathematics and Other Logical Essays.
      London: Kegan Paul, Trench, Trubner & Co., Ltd.; New York:
      Harcourt Brace and Co., 1931; Reprinted: New York: Humanities
      Press, 1950.
      An important essay on the Tractatus, by the distinguished young
      mathematical logician familiar with Wittgenstein, is among the
      papers contained in this posthumous book. The paper was origi-
      nally published as a Critical Notice in Mind, Vol. XXXII, No.
      128 (October 1923), pp. 465-478.

      Rhees, R. "Miss Anscombe on the Tractatus," The Philosophical
      Quarterly, Vol. 10, No. 38 (January 1960), pp. 21-31.
      A long and able review, generally favorable, of Miss Anscombe's An
      Introduction to Wittgenstein's Tractatus. "Sense" and "truth"
      are the chief concepts discussed.

      Russell, Bertrand. My Philosophical Development, With an Appendix,
      "Russell's Philosophy," by Alan Wood. New York: Simon and
      Schuster, 1959.
      Contains a frank account, however lacking in detail, of the in-
      tellectual relations between Russell and Wittgenstein in the
      latter's formative years, helping to throw some light upon the
      composition of the Tractatus.

      Ryle, Gilbert. "Books," Scientific American, Vol. 197, No. 3 (Sep-
      tember 1957).
      Ostensibly a review of Wittgenstein's Remarks on the Foundations
      of Mathematics, but actually a quick survey of much of the
      earlier work.

      ___. "Ludwig Wittgenstein," Analysis, Vol. 12, No. 1 (October,
      1951).
      A memorial, giving a short account of the philsoopher's direct
      contribution to contemporary thought.

"A Logical Mystic" (signed by S.). The Nation and the Athenaeum
    (January 27, 1923).
    A review of the Tractatus, done by someone awed by the style
    of the book, and not caring to work out any of the diffi-
    culties. This is interesting as an early estimate of the book
    before so many standard questions (e.g. whether Wittgenstein
    was a positivist, whether a "second Wittgenstein" succeeded
    the author of the Tractatus, and so on) became the stock-in-
    trade of so many writers. S. is plainly not a professional
    philosopher, but this, up to a point, is no disadvantage in
    reading the work of a man who clearly is one without always
    wishing to be thought so.

Schlick, Moritz. "The Future of Philosophy," Publications in
    Philosophy, edited and published by College of the Pacific,
    1932.
    A reworking of ideas contained in an article of the same title
    in the Proceedings of the Seventh International Congress of
    Philosophy. Either version is important as representing an
    early positivist interpretation of part of the Tractatus,
    mostly 4.112, and one which has given rise to many intellectual
    stereotypes. Much reprinted.

Shwayder, D. S. "=," Mind, Vol. LXV, No. 257 (January 1956),
    pp. 16-37.
    Question of identity and the equality discussed in terms of
    Wittgenstein, Frege, Russell and others.

____. "Wittgenstein's Tractatus; A Historical and Critical Com-
    mentary." (An unpublished dissertation for the D. Phil. degree
    at Oxford University, on file at the Bodleian Library.)
    This very long book is probably the best so far on the
    Tractatus, even though the author has indicated that he in-
    tends to make many changes before regular publication. Nobody
    seems to have grasped the Tractatus as a whole so well, and
    nobody has pursued its argument into the minutest details so
    deeply.

Stenius, Erik. Wittgenstein's Tractatus: A Critical Exposition of
    Its Main Lines of Thought. Oxford: Basil Blackwell, 1960.
    A systematic study, taking with considerable literalness many
    of Wittgenstein's remarks about logical space, imaging, and
    so forth, but attracting attention to much that is philo-
    sophical, rather than purely linguistic, in the text.

Stern, J. P. Lichtenberg, A Doctrine of Scattered Occasions.
    Bloomington: University of Indiana Press, 1959.
    Several parallels between Lichtenberg and Wittgenstein are
    mentioned.

(unsigned) "The Passionate Philosopher," The Times Literary Sup-
    plement, Friday, May 1, 1959, pp. 249-50.
    Mainly a review of the books by Anscombe and Malcolm on Witt-
    genstein, but containing some dissenting, independent opinions
    as well.

Urmson, J. O. Philosophical Analysis. Oxford: Clarendon Press,1956.
    A review of the early logical atomism of Russell, its effect
    upon Wittgenstein's Tractatus, and an account of succeeding
    positions.

Van Peursen, C. A. "Edmund Husserl and Ludwig Wittgenstein,"
    Journal of Philosophy and Phenomenological Research, Vol. XX
    (September 1959), pp. 181-95.

228   Warnock, G. J. _English Philosophy Since 1900_. London: Oxford
University Press, 1958.
The first two sections concern the _Tractatus_, and contain
a straightforward account of some of its chief tendencies.

Weiler, Gershon. "On Fritz Mauthner's Critique of Language," _Mind_,
Vol. LXII, No. 265 (January 1958).
An informative exposition of Mauthner's thought and its relation to the _Tractatus_, which throws light on why Wittgenstein
wished both to recall and dissociate himself from Mauthner.

Weinberg, Julius R. _An Examination of Logical Positivism_. London:
Routledge & Kegan Paul Ltd., 1950.
A book which happily displays more feeling for theses and the
structure of arguments in the _Tractatus_ than one ordinarily
finds in expositions. The author, like Urmson and Feibleman,
is concerned to show the multiple relationships between Wittgenstein and the Vienna positivists.

Wittgenstein, Ludwig. "Notes on Logic," _The Journal of Philosophy_,
Vol. LVI, No. 9 (April 25, 1957), pp. 280-345. With introduction
by Harry T. Costello. Early forerunner by Wittgenstein of the
Tractatus. The text of this "draft" has in part been publicly
questioned, but has nevertheless been reprinted by the
questioners in Wittgenstein's _Notebooks 1914-1916_.

_____. _Notebooks 1914-1916_. Edited by G. H. von Wright and G. E. M.
Anscombe with an English translation by G. E. M. Anscombe,
New York: Harper & Brothers, 1961.
This little volume contains much that became the _Tractatus_ a
few years later, and also much that was dropped. A number of
important remarks appear in several versions.

_____. _Logisch-Philosophische Abhandlung_. First published in _Annalen
der Naturphilosophie_, Vol. XIV (1921), pp. 185-262.

_____. _Tractatus Logico-Philosophicus_, with an Introduction by
Bertrand Russell. New York: Harcourt, Brace and Company; London:
Kegan Paul, Trench, Trubner, and Company, 1922. Reprinted 1933,
1947, 1949, 1951, 1955 (with an index by Max Black).
In this, the original text in German is printed with the translation, which is by C. K. Ogden with the help of Frank P. Ramsey.
The Introduction was written some time after Russell had lost
sympathy with Wittgenstein's doctrine. The index by Black in
later reprintings is not a full one.
    It has become almost customary, though not obligatory, to
take note of the fact that the Ogden translation is misleading.
This is true in many, many passages, no doubt, but a first
version of so difficult a work as the _Tractatus_ is bound to have
shortcomings. As a rule, really good translations do not come
along until the experience of many scholars has accumulated,
though Wittgenstein was luckier in the translations of his
other (and posthumously published) writings. In spite of its
weaknesses, there are many renderings by Ogden that can scarcely
be bettered, except in the most picayune details, such as slight
changes of punctuation. The greatest trouble in his translation
is in the complex of terms like picturing, presenting, representing, symbolizing, signifying, and so forth, where the distinctions
made by Wittgenstein are badly blurred in the English. For many
other paragraphs, although there may be good argument in favor
of a different reading, Ogden is close enough to make clear the
intent of the author. And at any rate, Ogden's version is the
one that has set the tone for all English-speaking commentators;
their departures are verbal, for the most part, and improve only
a little upon his capturing of the style and constructions.

____. Tractatus Logico-Philosophicus, with a new translation by
D. F. Pears and B. F. McGuinness. New York: The Humanities
Press, 1961.
This comes closer than Ogden's version to the original text. It
is new, say the translators, and not merely a correction of the
Ogden work, although in a surprising number of passages the
divergencies are very trifling. The chief objection to it is
in the number of reifications which Pears and McGuinness allow
to remain in their renderings; and there are certain places, as
in 5.133, "Alles Folgern geschieht a priori," where a rendering
other than "All deductions are made a priori" could have re-
vealed the exact meaning that Wittgenstein evidently had in
mind. But the translation is very good, and we are only sorry
that it appeared too late for us to take it into fuller account
in the Index.

____. Tractatus Logico-Philosophicus, Testo originale, versione
italiana a fronte, introduzione critica e note a cura di
G. C. M. Colombo, S. J. Milano" Fratelli Bocca, 1954.
A faithful Italian translation of the Tractatus, preceded and
followed by a number of explanatory essays. Colombo puts
Wittgenstein in a Positivist setting.

____. "Some Remarks on Logical Form," Proceedings of the Aristo-
telian Society, Supplement, Vol. IX, (1929), pp. 162-171.
The last - some would say the first - published work by Wittgenstein which shows close affiliations with the procedures of the
Tractatus, although it raises slightly different problems.

____. Letter to Mind, Vol. XLII, No. 167 (July 1933), pp. 415-416.
A sharp letter to the Editor asserting that Wittgenstein's own
doctrines were in constant flux. Taking him at his word, we
omit references here to the Blue & Brown Books, Philosophical
Investigations, and the rest, as being likely to distract
attention from the text we have been considering.